Copyright ©

All rights reserved

The characters and events portrayed in this book are based upon actual events. The Author has changed all the names of everyone in the book with the exception of his family. The true name of historical figures, saints, priests, and nuns have not been changed.

No part of this book may be reproduced, or stored in a retrieval system, or transmitted in any form or by any means, electronic, mechanical, photocopying, recording, or otherwise, without express written permission of the publisher.

ISBN: 9798363393655

Cover design by: Kelli MacPhail Gómez, et al.
Library of Congress Control Number: pending
Printed in the United States of America
RJB Publisher, Albuquerque, New Mexico
1935RJB@gmail.com

CONTENTS

Copyright
PREFACE
INTERIOR SOLDIER OF CHRIST
Prologue
 FOREWORD
Introduction

Seeds of Faith	1
Faith by Hearing	3
The Joy of Youth	7
The Sisters of St Francis	10
Saved from Drowning	13
Earthen Vessels	16
Lost Friendship	19
Mary's Grotto	21
Discrimination	23
You're in the Army Now	26
Battle Training	30
Across the Pacific	33
Tokyo Rose & Charlie	37
A Cry for Help	39
Lost in the Jungle	41

Bravery Under Fire	44
Moonlight Rosary	47
The Sign of the Cross	49
The Lonely Road	51
Death on the Mountain	54
The Crying Soldier	56
The 30 Day Mission	58
Squad Leader	61
Recruits and Mental Cases	63
Death in a Foxhole	67
The Grassy Hill	70
The Leyte Campaign	71
Fierce Combat	72
A Tropical Illness	75
Battle of Cebu-Goshen Hill	77
Sad News From Home	79
A Strange Country	81
A Soldier Returns Home	84
She Said "Yes"	87
Marriage and Family	89
An Unknown Path	91
Joining the Carmelite Order	93
Two Orders of Carmel	95
A Sunset Monastery	97
The Carmel Guild	99
Moving North	101
Vatican II	103
A New Home for the Third Order	105

The Discalced Carmelites	106
The Secular Order of Carmel	109
St. Therese of Lisieux	111
Silent Prayer and Lectio Divina	113
Devotion to St Joseph and Relics of St Therese	116
Mental Illness	120
On the Road	123
Moving Forward	126
Carmel and the Diaconate	128
Spiritual Warfare Contemplative Prayer	129
St. Teresa's Vision	134
Applying For the Diaconate	136
The Dark Mountain	138
Death of Connie	141
Ordination	143
The Great Parish Robbery	150
EPILOGUE	155
Back Cover Commentary	157
AFTERWARD	159
BIBLIOGRAPHY	161
About the Author	165

PREFACE

Deacon Ruben J. Barela, OCDS

The Infantry Division I fought with was the 23rd Division but had the nickname of Americal. It was formed in New Caledonia a French Island in the South Pacific in an emergency on 27th May 1942. I believe those in charge added the letter "L" to represent New Caledonia.

There is one thing we all have in common, and that is our faith in God and our Church, fundamental spiritual elements that carried us through many perilous moments of hostility. I offer my experiences in combat in the hope, perhaps, that they will encourage current and future veterans to remain faithful to God in time of peril. I do not force my beliefs on anyone, but there are many soldiers, sailors, pilots, lay people who live hidden lives serving others working quietly. I believe that this story has world -wide appeal due to its human flavor. However, I must add, that the wars of today are much different than those of yester year.

What I mean by this distinction is that contemporary conflicts often involve civilians, women, children, families - who get caught up in the crossfire of warfare.... collateral damage, I believe, is the modern term. Before, in my day, the lines between combatants were more clearly defined. Soldiers of today are in constant danger from the most unlikely roots. The very military personnel with whom they are fighting side-by-side, giving their all to obtain for these countries the freedom and democracy we enjoy and cherish, are often the enemy in their midst. I went into combat influenced by war movies, which were popular for boys and young men, in the early 1940's. They gave us a sense of excitement and of being unafraid of danger. However, I later learned from personal witness of death all around, how to begin to fear that I might not come home alive. In the wars of today modern technology and science have made dangerous strides that can wipe out entire countries with one bomb. What we need is faith, hope and charity. We need the help of our Blessed Mother to conquer evil with good.

It is important that I begin this journey as a story of faith and where that spiritual element originated, in the hope that it will encourage today's fighting young men and women, no matter which branch of service, that they are not alone, that God is always with them, if they just turn to Him, as I did many decades ago in the wars of the Pacific. Even as I write this, feeling very imperfect in many ways, I am assured that trusting God will always lead toward the right path as He certainly led and sustained me in those perilous times.

INTERIOR SOLDIER OF CHRIST

FIDELITY ON THE FRONT LINES

Deacon Ruben J. Barela, OCDS

Copyrighted

All Rights Reserved

Soldier Graphics By
Kelli MacPhail Gómez; Minnie P. Dávila; Brookelyn Resecker

PROLOGUE

I have written this book at the suggestion of my Pastor Father William Young Jr., of Queen of Heaven Parish in Albuquerque, New Mexico. He found out that there were three Veterans of World War II in the parish, and he wanted for each one of us to do a presentation of some experience in the War to present to the Parish on Veteran's Day on or about the year 2015. One of the Veteran's, a prisoner of the Nazis during the war did not want to talk about it. The other was a sailor who was in the Navy, but because of illness went to an Assisted Living Home. This is a true story of my Hidden Life with Christ. The names of my fellow soldiers have been changed to protect their privacy. Our life will bear fruit only if it is lived in Christ, but to see my whole life with its failures and victories seems to embrace a whole mystery that I will understand only in eternity. Most of my stories conclude with a quote from Scripture to connect and harmonize with my faith journey.

My journey in the military took me to several islands: New Caledonia, Bougainville, Leyte, Cebu and to Japan. Each one added to my education and experience of foreign lands that I never expected. I met people with strange customs and language that took time to learn some words, and their way of life.

I found the Japanese language the most difficult to understand. In the Philippines some of the people spoke Spanish which I speak. Some of the people spoke English, and others their own tribal language. There is much to learn from people with different customs, and to appreciate their history. The upshot of this is that even in war we can learn from each other.

FOREWORD

BARELA AWARDED

Pfc. Ruben J. Barela, 1609 Virginia Boulevard, was recently awarded the Bronze Star Medal for meritorious achievement against the Japanese. He is serving with an infantry division in the Southwest Pacific.

R. Barela

Albuquerque Journal, 1945

This then, is a true account of my early life, a chronical of experiences in World War II as an infantry foot-soldier, squad leader and radio operator, of my vocations of marriage, and service to God as a Deacon in the Catholic Church, complemented by membership in the Secular Order of Discalced Carmelites.

Commentary

This book covers the true life of faith for a small-town boy growing up in Albuquerque, New Mexico. At age four he is placed into a catholic orphanage, due to poverty and the death of his father. Exposed to the generosity and compassion of the nuns who ran the orphanage he develops an unshakable love for

Christ. His faith gives him the strength to endure the trials of warfare throughout World War II. His service involves being lost in enemy territory and momentarily being listed as "Missing in Action." In recognition of his heroism in battle he is awarded the Bronze Star. He ends his service by returning to his hometown, and there he begins a business, marries, raises a family, and becomes a Deacon of the Catholic Church.

In describing the battles fought in Bougainville and the Philippines it becomes evident that the attributes needed to succeed in spiritual warfare are identical to those needed in battle.

He details his spiritual battles. Each with eternal consequences. His enemies are fierce, invisible, and tempting twenty- four-hours a day. As he continues to mature in faith he must deal with an empty nest and death of his wife. He becomes a member of the Secular Carmelites and is ordained a Deacon of the Catholic Church. It is through servitude that his faith ultimately plateaus.

Paul Barela

INTRODUCTION

Kelli MacPhail Gómez; Minnie P. Dávila; Brookelyn Resecker

This story not only details his time in war, but also examines his religious journey from orphan to Deacon. This humble account is autobiographical and, is a recollection of real events. Research of past newspaper archives has helped to support his narrative.

While now retired, he continues to inspire and motivate his community to follow a life of faith based on his example. He is ninety-nine years old and still preaching at Mass on the second Sunday of the month. He serves as Spiritual Chaplain of the Catholic Daughters of the Americas Court # 2310 at Queen of Heaven Church in Albuquerque New Mexico, and Spiritual Assistant to the Secular Carmelites of John of the Cross Community With the help of God will continue to serve.

By Stephen Barela

Honorable Discharge

I provide further military groundwork, and offer the following from my Honorable Discharge Document, received at my separation ceremony in December 1945 at Fort Bliss, El Paso, Texas, U.S. Army base. It declares that I entered the military on

May 5, 1943, and following requisite infantry training, served in the Northern Solomon Islands in the Asiatic Pacific Theatre; that my duties included:

"Rifleman under extreme combat conditions, firing the rifle to destroy enemy personnel and assisting in the capture of enemy positions; all the while utilizing hand grenades and participating in close-quarter bayonet warfare."

It further states that I received the U.S. Army's Good Conduct Medal, Victory Medal and The Bronze Star, a decoration awarded to members of the U.S. Armed Forces for "heroic achievement, heroic service, meritorious achievement, or meritorious service in a combat zone."

SEEDS OF FAITH

Chapter 1

I was born on a farm near Albuquerque in December 1923 to Mariano Barela, and Candelaria Marie Garcia. I was the sixth of seven children, four boys and three girls. Their names: Mary, Amanda, Arthur, Alfonso, Eddie, Ruben, and Edwina. My twin brother Eddie came in a few minutes before me. I received My Lord Jesus Christ in baptism at San Felipe Neri Church in the Old Town neighborhood, just a few days after my birth. San Felipe Neri Church is one of the oldest in America. San Felipe Neri was known as the Apostle of Rome for his great wisdom and as a man of prayer. This beautiful Church honors him for his service to the Church.

Our mom tried her best raising such a large group of young children on her own while working full-time as an elevator operator. She first enrolled us in a nearby elementary school, where I began my education in first and second grade. However, she soon realized she could not tend to and support all our basic needs alone.

After a time of stress and worry - and I might add, much prayer - she was able to obtain help from the sisters of St. Francis at their Saint Anthony's Orphanage located on Indian School Road in the Northwest sector of the city. She was invited by the nuns to entrust my two brothers and me into their care. The other four siblings, my oldest brother and the three girls, remained at home. Saint Anthony's became our home from 1927 through 1935.

For me it meant from age four to nine, and it was a difficult time and painful for three young boys, having to leave home at such an early age, and only time would heal our situation. Life in the orphanage included going to daily Mass which led to me becoming an Altar Server, and serving at Mass was, and is, a special honor and great privilege in the Catholic Church, especially for young boys. The primary role of the altar server is to assist at the celebrant of the Holy Mass, by lighting the candles, with the washing of hands before the Consecration of the bread and wine and ringing the bells at the appropriate time and other duties. All servers, during Mass, must wear a white Alb. Things are very different now than when I served many years ago because the Mass was said in Latin, and I learned the prayers to be said at the foot of the Altar. There was a communion railing in front of the Altar to separate the people from the Sanctuary, and the priest had his back to the congregation. It is called the "Traditional" Mass and is celebrated in some Churches with permission from the bishop. For those of you reading this book, and are not familiar with the Mass, I will explain in another chapter. The title of this first chapter is "Seeds of Faith." Faith is a gift from God. Our Catholic Church expresses its faith in God by The Nicene Creed that we pray at Mass, and by living a life of faith by example.

"Faith is man's response to God, who reveals himself and gives himself to man, at the same time bringing man a superabundant light as he searches for the ultimate meaning of his life."[1]. As a Catholic I believe in the truths that Gods has revealed through his Church.

FAITH BY HEARING

Chapter 2

The nuns, who I learned to love, instilled in me the Seed of Faith. I still remember their names, Sister Judith, Principal, and Sister Rosita and Sister Socorro, both teachers. By going to Mass daily, I began to listen to the Word of God. To believe the Word we must listen. Residing in this new home was not easy, especially living side-by-side with 300 other boys, some much older than my brothers and me. A few of them were arrogant and did not treat the sisters with respect; others were constantly ready for a good fight. By the time I reached third grade, I had already been in several scuffles defending my twin brother. Of course, the adage "boys will be boys" may be appropriate in this case. Most of the boys were well behaved and appreciated the Nuns.

Life at St. Anthony's paralleled the regular Public-School year, so summer vacations were spent at home. During that time, my brothers and I were able to look for work, mostly selling newspapers and doing other odd jobs. Al, my older brother hung around with older kids. We occupied our idle time playing football and baseball with other boys in the neighborhood. Believe it or not our football games as kids were as rough as those played by professional adults today. We played without grass or turf as they do. It is known as "sandlot" football. We did not have interference calls or all the other rules that they have today, and we came out of the game with knee bruises and sore arms and legs and dirt all over. We took our games seriously because we were playing teams from other sections of the city.

We lived about a mile from the newspaper publishing facility, so we had to leave our house daily at 5:00 a.m. to arrive on time to get our allotment of papers and, the manager assigned the delivery circuits. There was stiff competition for the best street corners with stronger sales possibilities. Nonetheless, it was obvious to us that the manager favored a boy who was always assigned a good spot in front of the Court Café, which was a busy breakfast restaurant where many newspapers could be sold. The daily editions sold for three cents, and we were given one cent for each one and the publishing company got two. The Sunday paper sold for twenty-five cents and, as I recall, we were able to make seven cents on each of those sales. Our shares seemed like skimpy amounts, but at that time bread was only five cents, while milk and other essential items were similarly low in cost. The barber only charged twenty- five cents. In the winter we searched for firewood for our wood stove from the sawmill about a half mile away from home. Some of the other boys had to look for firewood also. The sawmill was a private company with a large fence around it and we went there at night looking for firewood in the cold winter for our stoves to keep the house warm. They had a guard that went around the property to keep intruders out, but we waited until he went out of sight to gather some small pieces of wood. He would fire warning shots if he saw anyone trying to get wood.

The important result of our adventure into the business world was that we made great and long-lasting friendships. Recently one of those life-long friends died. We had kept in touch over the years. Mostly at Church functions as he was a devout Catholic. I always wanted to be as devout as he was. His friendship surfaced much later in life as we both served the Church.

Toward my latter years at the orphanage, I was able to receive two of the most important Sacraments of the Catholic Church, First Holy Communion and Confirmation. One providential - perhaps milepost in my life occurred the day after my first Holy Communion. Sister Rosita was passing out holy pictures to the class, beginning with the students who sat in the front, and I could see that they were beautiful, except for one that was plainly undistinguished. As the she came forward toward me, I hoped for a picture of the Sacred Heart of Jesus. Instead, she gave me the one that I did not prefer. It was of the Virgin Mary. I was disappointed. I was too young to know the beauty and holiness of the Virgin Mary. I will later relate how this picture gave me consolation in the war. We were also given a prayer book that I treasured all my life until by mistake I left it in the pew of a Church. Amid all this action we believe as Saint Paul says:

"Thus, faith comes from what is heard, and what is heard comes through the word of Christ"[2]

Picking Piñons

One of our neighbors had a Model "T" Ford that it had to be cranked for it to start much like the old- style airplanes with a propeller that had to be started by hand. It took us at least four hours to travel about thirty miles. We went through the only highway that led to the mountains, and into the Tijeras Canyon. The Sandia Mountains are huge and at that time there were many bears and mountain lions and mountain goats that roamed the area. The area leading to the mountains was desert full of tumble weeds dry bushes and, all kinds of snakes and other desert creatures. New Mexico receives eight inches of rain a year according to the Weather Service. There was only one house in the distance with a windmill for drawing water, and the windmill could be seen from a distance. It was the only sign that there were people around in this deserted place.

The driver had to put water in the radiator every ten miles or so. The purpose of our trip was to pick piñons, and we spent all day doing that. Our parents took sack lunches and we managed to pick enough piñons to last us for the winter. It was hard work getting on our knees to pick them, but it was fun being in the mountains. On the way back I kept looking at the windmill in the distance and wondered who lived in such isolation far away from the city.

But now in retrospect, I have a better idea of how being away from the city crowd can be a blessing. Spiritual writers speak of how the desert has much to teach us. Jesus fasted and prayed in the desert, and in the mountains. The Bible speaks of how Israelites traveled for forty years through the Sinai Desert before arriving at the Promised Land.

THE JOY OF YOUTH

Chapter 3

When we first moved to the city from the farm, the population of Albuquerque was about thirty-five thousand, and we lived on Virginia Boulevard in a house about a mile north of the main highway at the time called Route 66 or Central Avenue. Our home had a living room, three bedrooms, a porch, and a cellar. It was big enough for our family because one of our sisters had married and moved to her own residence. Initially we attended North Fourth Street School, which was close to home and, where I attended first and second grades; my twin brother Eddie was a year behind me in studies.

It is remarkable that at that age romance begins to grow in a small child, but some of my friends, made fun of me and said: "ha, ha, Ruben loves Lillian." Lillian was in my class, and I did like her, and she seemed to like me. I also had a friend that came from the East side of the mountains, and we hung around together and had a great time. I do not know if his family took him to our school since the distance was about twenty miles away. My point is that he stopped coming and I missed him. It was a true friendship between two young boys, and I felt sad when he did not return. I kept waiting and hoping that he would return, but he never came back. I waited on the playground for him, but he never returned, and I was sad for a long time.

Mother had registered the family as parishioners at Immaculate Conception Catholic Church, a downtown Jesuit parish, about a mile walk from where we lived. To attend Mass, we made the trek every Sunday. It took my mom a year or two before she found work. She worked as an elevator operator for the city and an older sister worked at St. Anthony's Orphanage. We were poor, but happy.

The name "Immaculate Conception" refers to the Virgin Birth of Mary. There is a description of her birth in a prophecy by the Prophet Isaiah. God had asked King Ahab through the Prophet to ask for a sign, but he refused. "Therefore: "the Lord himself will give you this sign: the virgin shall be with child, and bear a son, and shall name him Immanuel." [3]

The Crash of 29

The Market Crash of 1929 was a bad time for the whole country. We were not the only ones that were poor. We saw neighbors struggling to make end meet. My brother Arthur got a job with the WPA a government project that provided work for the country planting trees, improving highways and other important jobs. But the pay was one dollar a day. I also remember unloading heavy bags of potatoes from a railway car. The bags weighed fifty pounds and we were paid a penny a bag. Arthur and I were assigned by mom to pick up flour and eggs at the Welfare Center. My brother Alfonso and Eddie did not want to be seen at the Welfare Center. I did not like it either, but it had to be done for us to have food. It was as an adult that I learned how devastating was the Market Crash of 1929, and how it affected the Stock Market and the economy. It took several years for the country to recover, but our situation did not change much. We still were in the lower bracket as wage earners.

Milking Cows

We had a friend of the family who worked at the dairy farm, and he invited me to learn how to milk cows. I was hesitant, but then decided to do it. I had to get up early in the morning to do that kind of work. This was a large farm providing the community with milk, ice cream and other produce. I was still young, and he told me to watch him at his trade. He grabbed a bucket sat on a small stool and began to milk the cows by hand. The cows were lined up in a stall one next to the other in a barn eating hay as he milked them. He said: "look out for the tail", but the tail of the cow kept striking my face, as I tried to milk them. "Be gentle and watch out for the tail." he repeated. It is hard work and requires some skill to milk cows, but I did help him a couple more times. The milk was put into clean aluminum cans for later distribution. Today, machines do the work of milking cows, but then I learned something new, and thank God for dairy farmers. The upshot I did get to drink fresh milk. God created all the animals for our needs. "God remembered Noah and all the animals, wild and tame, that were with him in the Ark" [4]

Lick the Spoon

During the hot summer an ice cream vendor came through the neighborhood streets in a horse-drawn wagon selling his many varieties of that frozen and delicious ice cream. Funny thing about this working man is that every time he sold a scoop of ice cream on a cone, he would lick the spoon. It got to the point where we began calling him in Spanish, "lambe la cuchara," or "lick the spoon" in English.

On one occasion the wagon came close to our house while the kids were yelling "here comes "lambe la cuchara." The commotion caused the horse to spook and buck, resulting in the wagon overturning on the street, and the entire load of ice cream fell out, and there was little anyone could do, as the horses were dangerous to approach, so "lambe" told us to help ourselves. We all felt sorry for him but enjoyed the sudden feast of free ice cream in all flavors. It took many hours for them to clean up the street and calm down the horses, but he came back the next day with a new wagon and "Lick the Spoon" was happy and so were we. This story will appear again in the latter part of my life. Again, we have animals serving mankind, two horses helping to deliver ice cream to the poor.

THE SISTERS OF ST FRANCIS

Chapter 4

The sisters at the orphanage belonged to a Religious Order named The Sisters of St. Francis. They sacrificed their lives to serve others. They were from Mishawaka, Indiana. They staffed St. Anthony's Orphanage, in Albuquerque, until 1971.[5]

There were about eight sisters, and each had their own work to do, some were teachers, others were cooks, others worked in the infirmary. There were two lay women who helped with some of the chores. They were not perfect but living in an enclosed community can be difficult at times. I found them to be happy, although some of the kids were unruly and gave the sisters a bad time.

The Razor Blades

The building had stairwells leading to the upper floors. The floors were varnished but with constant use the varnish was wearing out. The one way the sisters decided to solve the problem was to have the boys use razor blades to scrape off the old varnish. We did it step by step, and it took many days to finish the job, but we got it done, and the sisters were happy. Sometimes we had to clean the big yard where we played and clean the swimming pool. We had games, for example, a contest for the best swimmer and best pitcher and batter in baseball.

St. Anthony's Orphanage was surrounded on the West by

wilderness, one residence, and a forest with no paved roads. In fact, the only road leading to the orphanage was also un-paved it was a graveled road. The main building had three stories which included dormitories for the boys, assigned according to age. Another section housed classrooms and a large dining room, and a building that housed everything needed for maintenance. In addition, there was an infirmary in case of illness. The entire complex was like a small city within itself but surrounded by wooded areas and the Rio Grande a short distance away. Most of the children would go to the forest near the river and hunt for berries that were delicious, and they also carried small sling shots to shoot down birds. They kept count of the number killed to see who would kill the most. It is not a good thing to talk about, but they had time on their hands during the Summer, and they engaged in something that was not good.

I recall that while sitting at our desks at class we could see apples through the windows growing in an orchard. They were big and ripe, but we were not allowed access the orchard or its delicious fruit. All we could do was look at them and hope for a chance to be given one of the apples. The orphanage did provide three meals a day for the 300 residents. There were many times when we got apples as desert at meals.

In the morning, after Mass, we went to the dining room and sat with our classmates, and ate breakfast consisted of oatmeal and peanut butter mixed with syrup that we could put on our bread. It was delicious. So much so, that I still duplicate that morning meal in my adulthood. For lunch we usually had a meat entrée and vegetables. And for dinner, most often we were served macaroni and cheese. I often went without dinner because I could not stand mac cheese.

One of our regular chores was accompanying one of the nun's door-to-door in Albuquerque neighborhoods, asking for donations for the orphanage. I went with one of the sisters on occasion. Another responsibility the students had was participating in funerals, processing to the local cemetery, called Mount Calvary, to attend the burial of an infant or someone with little or no family. The cemetery was about a mile and a half away. The nuns made sure we were dressed in our Sunday best for these occasions. I was very much afraid of death and tried not to think about the person being interred. For those who are not familiar with the word "Mass" it is the celebration of the sacrifice of Christ on Calvary in an unbloody manner. "At the Last Supper Jesus anticipated the free offering of his life."

"On the eve of his passion, while still free, Jesus transformed this Last Supper with the apostles into the memorial of his voluntary offering to the Father for the salvation of men" "This is my body which is given up for you." "This is my blood which is poured for many for the forgiveness of sins."[6] The Nuns gave excellent example of reverence for the Mass and the priest.

SAVED FROM DROWNING

Chapter 5

Once at a baseball game, when I was assigned to play catcher, one of the batters, after hitting the ball, flung the bat backwards, and hit me in the head causing a gash above my left eye, accompanied by much bleeding. I was taken to the infirmary for treatment and for many years had a scar to prove I had been wounded playing catcher in an orphanage baseball game.

There was an older classmate whose parents apparently had some clout because he received the daily morning paper, and during recess many of the boys crowded around him to find out what had happened to Tim Tyler, who was a hero in the funnies who got into all kinds of trouble in the jungles of Africa. The daily comic strips carried battles between tigers and other jungle beasts and Tim was in the middle of it all.

The Runaway Truck

The sisters had everything under control as we lived by "the bell." Every time that bell rang, we knew to gather in line for the next class or meeting. They had arrangements for our haircuts at one of Barber Shops downtown. We went by truck and, were packed like sardines on an old truck, on our way over the driver of the rickety truck was driving erratically. The truck was old and the boards on the side of the truck were old and loose. When he turned corners, we would all swing from one side to the other.

It was scary as we had no control over our bodies as we went from side to side and packed like sardines. We made it to the shop and got our haircuts, but on the way back he drove just as fast and turning a street corner, we all fell out onto the street. Some were hurt bad and were taken to the Infirmary and others had bruises and sore arms and legs. I had a few bruises and do not want to ever get on a car or truck with that driver.

The orphanage had a great swimming pool in which most of us learned to swim. Nearby there was a man-made lake, about an acre in size, near the pool. It belonged to a private sawmill business in which logs were dumped in preparation for lumber. On a few occasions we would sneak into the lake and get on the logs to roll them with our feet to see who could stay up the longest without falling into the water. It was a dangerous exercise and at times we fell into the water and struggled to regain control because as we tried to get back on the log it would roll, and the only way, we could get back on was to push it against another log and pray that we would not drown in that smelly water. I had the experience of almost drowning in this lake.

Much later when I left the Orphanage, I was swimming in a canal where many young people swam. It was called "The Rapids" because of its raging waters. I did not realize how strong the current was. It had a diving board, and I jumped into the water. I struggled against the rough water and started sinking. One of the expert swimmers saw me and jumped in to help me. If it was not for Dick, and our Blessed Mother, I would probably not be writing this story. He and his family lived only about a half-mile from us, and he knew me well. I also read in the book of John of the Cross that he was saved from drowning by the Blessed Mother.

This reminds me of Saint Peter as recorded in Mathew's Gospel. Jesus walks on the sea. "Then he made the disciples get into the boat and precede him to the other side, …When it was evening, he was there alone, meanwhile the boat, already a few miles off-shore, was being tossed about by the waves for the wind was against it. During the fourth watch of the night, he came toward them, walking on the sea 'when the disciples saw him walking on the sea, they were terrified. "It is a ghost," they said, and they cried out in fear. At once Jesus spoke to them, "Take courage, it is I, do not be afraid." Peter said to him in reply, "Lord, if it is you, command me to come to you on the water., He said, "come." Peter got out of the boat and began to walk on the water toward Jesus. But when he saw how [strong] the wind was he became frightened; and, beginning to sink, he cried out, "Lord, save me!" Immediately Jesus stretched his hand and caught him, and said to him, "O you of little faith, why did you doubt?" [7]

EARTHEN VESSELS

Chapter 6

Of course, we were not perfect students. Now and then, at night, we would creep out of the dormitory around bedtime, go down the fire escape and walk to downtown to see a movie. The price of movie tickets was ten cents. Some would ask their parents for money for the movie tickets when they visited. The sisters as, far as I know, never did know that we sneaked out after dark to go downtown,

The movies were the Western type and some of the actors were Tom Mix, Hoot Gibson, and Ken Maynard. John Wayne was beginning his career, and I remember one of his first Western movies was "Blue Steel." These movies were in a serial format and at the end of each one the main actor would be trapped by robbers or some such peril, and one had to see the next serial to see how he escaped. They were interesting for children. The Nuns did take us to a couple of movies while I was there. One of the movies was titled "Captains Courageous," and the other one, "Little Women." The first one was fun for us boys, but the latter one was more for the Nuns then for the boys.

<u>The Big Bully</u>

One of my friends was Mike. We always hung together after class. I was seven at the time and he was about eight. There was a big bully at the school and his name was Joe. Most were afraid of him because he was a tough one and everyone knew it. He had been in several fights, and no one was able to beat him. At every fight all the kids hung around to see who would win. But one day he got into an argument with my friend Mike, and they began a fist fight. At last Joe met his match. Mike had long arms and Joe was not able to get to many punches in. Mike kept him at bay while giving him jabs that began to hurt Joe. Joe did not give up but kept punching. I was rooting loud for Mike when an older fellow pushed me to the ground mad because I was favoring Mike. Fortunately, the bell sounded, and they stopped the fight, but I believe that Joe learned his lesson be careful who you pick on. I will relate later in my story about Mike.

The Donut Drama

When we first arrived at our new home, the orphanage, my twin brother Eddie was placed in a grade below me, even though he was a few minutes older. This was determined by the sister in charge. Alfonso was placed in a grade above. Both of my brothers, for reasons I did not understand, found the sisters unworthy of their respect, and showed it. The nuns had a difficult time distinguishing between me and Eddie as he looked very much like me. We were twin brothers, and at three o'clock in the afternoon it was donut time for the kids, and Sisters began serving donuts beginning with the First Grade. When the Third Graders came, I held my hand to receive my donut, but she would not give me one. She called me names such as greedy. She looked at me with scorn and called me dishonest. This happened two days in a row, and she refused to give me a donut, so I went without it. It was difficult for me as at that time kids get hungry. Later I told my brother to get in front of me, and when my time came for my donut, she said, aha, there's two of you." I thought that she would say something nice, and apologize, but she was not to be corrected. I cannot blame her she did not know I had a twin brother.

My brothers did not like the rules we were required to abide by. As I advanced in my studies, one of the nuns, Sister Socorro, had me do errands for her. I would deliver school paraphernalia and messages back and forth, from classroom to classroom, to the principal's office, or wherever she directed. I had a great respect for her and enjoyed doing the tasks she gave me. I sensed a worthy kinship developing between us. I liked the other sisters also, but she was very special.

LOST FRIENDSHIP

Chapter 7

That friendship suffered and virtually ended when my brother Eddie disobeyed Sister. Sister taught other classes, and she punished him for breaking the rules. The mistake for me was that I sided with him. She never called on me again for any chores and errands. I made a big mistake by supporting Eddie. From then on, I regretted turning against her, and. my action that day also emboldened Eddie to continue breaking rules. I left the orphanage after several years and to this day I still pray for Sister Socorro to forgive me. Later, as an adult, I tried to keep up with events at the orphanage, and often went to Mass there on my own, but I never saw Sister Socorro again. I have only memories of a beautiful friendship. We must treasure our friendships because we need each other. Jesus said to his disciples: "You are my friends, if you do what I command you." "I no longer call you slaves, because a slave does not know what his master is doing. I have called you friends..." [8]

Christmas at St. Anthony's

The Nativity celebration of our Lord was a very joyous event with the different classes held in the gymnasium at alternate times. The students loved receiving their gifts donated by local charitable organizations. Many of us wanted a harmonica because the older kids requested them. But the presents varied from marbles that were much in demand in those days, and others asked for kites they could fly in the big schoolyard. Once

I received a top, a small wooden cone-shaped toy that came with a strong string that one could wind around it then throw on the ground and watch It spin. The idea to see which top would spin for a longer time. You could also learn, from much practice, to pick it up between fingers and let it continue to spin in your hand.

But the best part of Christmas was the celebration of "Midnight Mass" I believe the celebrant of the Mass was Father Hartman. I cannot remember his first name. In Spanish, the Mass is known as "Misa del Gallo" in reference to the early morning crowing of some birds. Many family members came to the Mass, and I was happy to see my mom and sisters. The morning was followed by delicious foods at breakfast. The Birth of Christ is celebrated all over the world. "Jesus was born in a humble stable into a poor family. Simple shepherds were the first witnesses to this event. In this poverty heaven's glory was made man-fest." [9]

MARY'S GROTTO

Chapter 8

When at the Orphanage together with the sisters we went to the Volcano Cliffs as it was called then. The volcanos were across the Rio Grande about a mile away. We took a bus across the river and proceeded to the hills where there were three of these volcanos that had been dormant for thousands of years. The purpose of the jaunt was to gather volcanic rock for a Grotto to be built to honor the Virgin Mary. A grotto is a structure made to resemble a natural cave. As I recall there were no restrictions or prohibitions at that time for gathering rock from the volcanos or the mountains. We would work in shifts with the bigger boys to help build the grotto. It took a long time selecting the right stones to fit over another one and chipped away at others.

But the great day came when the work was completed and the whole school gathered with the priest, and the sisters to pray the rosary and honor the Virgin Mary, The Mother of God. We would gather once a week to pray at the grotto. Those were beautiful times, and I cannot forget them. Today the area of the volcanos is known as Petroglyph Park and no rocks can be removed.

The following is a photo of the grotto.

With the gathering of the students and the priest.

DEACON RUBEN BARELA

DISCRIMINATION

Chapter 9

My schooling, after the years at the orphanage, continued at then Washington Junior High, later called Washington Middle School, oldest of all middle schools in the city of Albuquerque. It was there I encountered conspicuous and unchecked discrimination toward Hispanic students. The standard operating policy was that all white students were assigned to classrooms together and Spanish likewise.

At a certain point while attending this school, but never knowing exactly why, I was moved from the Spanish class in with the white students. I speculated that perhaps one of the teachers might have complained that there should be some Spanish student in a "white" classroom, perhaps an attempt to pacify some of the parents since it was so discriminatory and unfair. Another Hispanic student as well, was transferred to the all-White class. His name was Willie. Thus, Willie and I became the only ones in an all-white class. The ethnic make-up of the school was about 50/50, or about even between Anglo and Hispanic students. I had blonde hair when a small boy, but it changed color to reddish as I grew older.

When I managed to wind up in a room with white kids, it was inevitable that someone would complain. So, when that complaint was lodged, I am not sure by whom, it caused moments of anxiety for Willie and me and, probably likewise for the teacher, and administration. I remember thinking it odd that we were not allowed to speak Spanish in the school or on the school grounds, yet in contradiction to that standard, discouraged even from mingling with the white students. As I recall, there was only one Hispanic on the school's basketball team, even though half the enrollees were Hispanic. On occasion there were even problems among the Spanish speakers. Once I had an argument with a Hispanic kid; he told me to meet him after school to settle the issue. Later, I waited for him at the designated spot, but he never showed up.

After Washington Junior High came Albuquerque High School where I attended class for three years, as a Sophomore, Junior, and Senior. There discrimination toward Hispanic students continued; as in junior high, we were denied the freedom to speak Spanish on school grounds under penalty of dismissal. I walked a mile every day to attend classes, since we were poor, I took a tortilla in my pocket for lunch. During recess in the morning a rich kid would eat pastries and made me hungry, but he would not share. Many years later as an adult I met this fellow again when I had my own business, and his dad ran a large Company. I bought articles from them, and I tried to convert him and told him that he had a soul within him to take care of, but he said, "If I have one it is not any good."

In May of 1943, during my senior year and at the age of 19, I decided to join the military just a couple of years after the attack on Pearl Harbor by the Japanese. Thus, World War II interrupted my high school education. Following my stint in the U. S. Army, I would return to classes to obtain my high school diploma, plus additional studies, secular and religious.

In summary and as I look back on my childhood what sticks in my mind mostly is that schism between Anglos and Hispanics, was a separation not just geographic but in language, culture and attitude. There was that constant and deep division that provoked violent encounters. Much later after World War II things began to change, and Hispanics and others began to slowly move to the Northeast Heights where most of the wealthy people lived.

The Kimo Theatre Fracas

I remember vividly one such incident. It came by word-of-mouth, that there would be a possibly turbulent confrontation by the two factions near The Kimo Theatre on a certain Saturday morning. The Kimo Theatre was located on the main street of town. When the day arrived a large group of Anglos appeared from the area called the Northeast Heights. Likewise, a sizable number of Hispanics from "the valley" gathered in front of the theatre too. After some angry exchanges of words, chaos started, and the battle began. It was a terrible fracas. Many boys charging at each their fists swinging in anger. In the melee, several boys were injured. I recall my brother Al throwing some punches at a white kid. It was the young girls who fortunately called the police, they were concerned about their boyfriends. The police broke it up, but not before many bloody noses and black eyes had been exacted in the process. When it was all over, nothing had been resolved. The fight ended in a draw and the indignities of racism continued to boil over on any number of future occasions. My story continues with family interests.

I recall when we were still young my brother Eddie and I were given the job of by one of our relatives of ringing a bell as we rode on the back of a truck as an election was going on for Governor of New Mexico. Tensions were high as the division between Anglos and Spanish was still going on. It was a cold winter, and our hands were freezing. The people in the truck were not aware that we were cold. I do not remember who won the election, but Eddie and I did our part.

Jesus says: "But to you who hear I say, love your enemies, do good to those who hate you, bless those who curse you, pray for those who mistreat you…do to others as you would have them do to you." [10]

YOU'RE IN THE ARMY NOW

Chapter 10

Upon enlisting in the U.S. Army as a volunteer - May 5, 1943 - I was inducted and transferred to a military installation in California, near the city of San Luis Obispo. It was called Basic Training for infantrymen and would last six months. The base had been built in 1940, as a World War II combat boot-camp. At its peak it housed 45,000 troops and was located on both sides of the Salinas River in Monterey and San Luis Obispo Counties. Originally called Camp Nacimiento Replacement Training Center, it was renamed Camp Roberts in honor of a World War I Congressional Medal of Honor recipient, Corporal Harold W. Roberts, who gave his life in "The War to End All Wars." His tank had become disabled during combat in France. He and his companion became trapped inside the vehicle, which had sunk in a hole full of water, from which only one could exit. Roberts assisted his companion's escape but remained inside and drowned. Other trainees arrived at Camp Roberts at the same time I did. We were assigned to an Army Barrack that had few creature comforts, a bare-bones building with wood floors and side-by-side cots for sleeping. We were supplied with olive drab garb; also, a hat, helmet, canteen, backpack. rifle, bayonet, combat boots, shoes and a brand-new nom-de-guerre buzz phrase, G.I., or "Government Issue," in other words, those who wore the green. We had obtained our badges at the Recruiting Center which introduced us to yet another well-known metaphorical label, "dog tags."

The first morning we awakened by a loud bugle call called Reveille a signal to get up in the morning. It is a bugle at about sunrise signaling the first military formation of the day. Any new soldier who delayed getting out of bed at its sound, invited the wrath of a sergeant who would flip the cots over, with soldiers still in them. I witnessed this a several times. Next, we lined up right outside the barrack while our names were called out. Some of them were strange to me; names I had never heard, from all kinds of different ethnicities. The new soldiers were from all over, New York, Texas, West Virginia, and other areas of the country. The bugle sound at night is called "taps" It is the last call of the night signaling that the lights will be turned off. Taps is also part of the ceremony at funerals and Memorial Services. Many priests and deacons officiate at these services. I have often assisted at funeral and the Committal services. It is one of the most solemn and rewarding gifts of God.

One of the reasons I volunteered for the Infantry was that a nephew had been killed in the desert of North Africa during combat against German forces under the command of General Rommel, popularly known as "The Desert Fox." My nephew, Robert, was a U.S. Army tank driver who died in action when his armored vehicle was hit by an anti-tank mortar. Allied forces were eventually victorious over the Rommel fighters, but my nephew's death in battle inspired me to want to follow his example. He was very much loved by those who knew him. He always played quarterback when we played football as kids. It was called "sandlot football."

I met many young men from colleges in California, New York, and other Eastern States. I remember an older man from New York who would tell us "Don't tell me anything I'm from New York" indicating that he was smarter than all of us. We had a good laugh at his dry humor.

Another was always eating candy bars even in the bathroom. My disposition was such that I was able to get along with all of them.

I was very thin and weighed 110 lbs., but when it came to climbing the tall obstacle courses on ropes I kept up and oftentimes beat the taller men. It was grueling to see who could climb up the high obstacle course and scale down on the other side. The officers kept track of statistics. It was competition at its best. These college men were strong and athletic. Not many men could keep up with them when it came to endurance.

<u>Basic Training</u>

"Boot Camp," lasted normally depending on the branch of service, anywhere from 16 to 26 weeks. Mine was the latter, a six - month period of intense and grueling infantry warfare exercises. It became a challenging period of backbreaking, exhaustive work, having to get up early each morning for calisthenics, followed by marching in unison and finally, classes on what to expect in combat.

The Sergeants-in-Charge were generally rough-and-tumble, mean taskmasters who pulled no punches. We were taught that in combat the choices we made were matters of life-and-death, not only for ourselves but for the army buddies at our side. It was simulated combat, but in many ways, real. The hardest part for me was crawling for long distances burdened by the heavy weight of fighting equipment on my back. In warfare we were told: "do something even if it's wrong."

Basic training recruits had to become familiar with a variety of firearms. The main ones to achieve proficiency in were: the M1 Garand Rifle; the M1918 B.A.R. (Browning Automatic Rifle), machine gun, the mortar, a simple, lightweight, portable, muzzle loaded weapon; and the Bazooka, a short-range tubular rocket launcher used against tanks, and the forty-five pistol for close fighting which I carried later as a radio operator.

At times we were subject to the wiles of the leaders; one needed to stay alert as to the motives and craftiness of these non-commissioned officers who were our trainers. We had to watch out for certain ones whose clever practices, in ways that exposed their desired expectations for the recruits they were responsible with forming into combat-ready fighters. An example I can describe because I remember it vividly was when one of the Sergeants asked of all his troops, "Do we have any experienced truck drivers here? If so, raise your hands." About four of them innocently gullible ones, figured they were going to get a neat job driving a truck, and responded. The Sergeant would select the hand-raisers and a little later we would observe the volunteers pushing wheel- barrows full of concrete, provoking chuckles from among those who had not taken the bait. They also had the phrase "kitchen police", and they would ask for volunteers. The volunteers did not realize that it meant peeling potatoes in the kitchen.

During my time at Camp Roberts, I was able to attend Mass on Sundays. It was joyful to meet others of the same faith as mine. There were other soldiers of a different faith practicing their faith on Sundays. There was little else of a spiritual nature, except for quiet time for private prayer and meditation, and was part of my interior life as a soldier of Christ. My stretch at this California base during summer was extremely hot. There was a small place where one could get a milk shake to cool down after duty if there was time. We marched daily on scorching asphalt and often one or more of the men would pass out from exhaustion.

BATTLE TRAINING

Chapter 11

Our training segments at Roberts encompassed learning about chemical warfare, including how to survive a gas attack. Upon entering the room where the gas was released, we had to move quickly to get our gas masks on. It could have been mustard gas, but not sure. It was a terrifying experience even though we had the masks to protect us. As soon as the gas was turned on, I could smell the horrible stench. It immediately became hard to breathe, even with the mask's protection; I thought I was going to pass out. We were locked in. It seemed like ages for the test to end and to be outside again. One of the recruits an older man broke out with severe burns on his face and had to be driven to the base hospital. It was rough, but all part of the training to learn how to stay alive in battle.

Dodging Real Bullets

The scariest thing for me in Basic Training was when we were ordered to slither on our bellies about one hundred yards to a bunker where a soldier was firing live bullets over our heads to simulate a real battle. We had to keep our heads down because of the danger. I could feel the bullets whistling over my head. All participants were glad when this part of our training was over. On another day, we had night training in the mountains. This mission was to rendezvous with another Company and engage them in a mock battle. But our lieutenant, who even though he had a compass to guide us got us lost in the night. We never found the other Company and as a result, got a poor score.

The Thirty-Six-Mile Hike

The other experience that has stayed with me all my life was a 36-mile hike through hot California roads and trails leading up into the mountains. The arduous trek began on Sunday morning at 2:00 a.m. with full field pack. By that I mean rifle, hand-grenades, bayonet, ammunition belt, canteen full of water and rations to keep us nourished during the march. We were told that anyone who dropped out would have to repeat the exercise later. The hike was meant to toughen us up for combat. We marched through the city and on to the side roads that would lead to the mountains.

Our Company was made up of about 200 men and as we marched through the city and on to the deserted roads, we sang songs to stay alert mostly military tunes we all had learned. One of the songs we sang was, "Bless them All, the long and the short and the tall." I do not know who wrote it, but we sang it. As daylight came, we found it hard to breathe because of the dust stirred up by the action of heavy boots pounding the ground. We were breathing the dust. Most of us covered our mouths with handkerchiefs to protect our lungs.

We were given breaks every few hours and that was a welcome respite. As time passed, marching-and-marching, it became monotonous and a struggle to keep up. We just kept singing and yearning for an end to the hike. After some time, we all became quiet to keep our strength up as the going got more difficult, it was a time of developing endurance, not for talk. And then as dusk began to appear, it became apparent that some would not be able to complete the mission. An army vehicle would pick up those who had collapsed.

I was getting more and more spent as the march continued. Ahead was a mountain that had to be scaled. I could go no further, so I went a little way from the road and sat down under a tree, while the remainder of the Company trekked on by. As I rested, I heard a noise in the distance, a celebration of sorts. I realized at that moment that I was only about a hundred yards from the end of the hike. I had made it to the end, but it was thirty-six hours I shall never forget. Best of all, it prepared me for the hardships of actual battle. Nonetheless, the real test of endurance would come later in the jungles of the South Pacific.

ACROSS THE PACIFIC

Chapter 12

Following the six months of brutal, sometime difficult, Basic Training, we had earned two weeks furlough to return home, visit family and prepare for the unknown. During my leave at home, I enjoyed being back with my family for two weeks, and I went to the horse races with my older sister and another young lady. I won a few bucks and bought a war bond to help the cause. It was a tearful parting with my family, especially with Mom, she could not hold back the tears, and my brother Arthur was sad, but they knew why I had to go. I reported to Fort Bliss in El Paso, a staging area, deploying from there to Seattle, Washington. None of us knew what might be in store for a bunch of rookie soldiers, but we would soon find out. This first stage of an unforgettable adventure began with a slow several days train ride from West Texas to the extreme Northwest port of Seattle, where we would be emplaced on a troop ship for a long journey to unknown regions of the world.

In Seattle we were taken to the port and introduced to a large, four-story-high, former cruise ship, that had been converted into a troop carrier. This ocean liner was built to accommodate about 1,000 vacationing passengers. After being redesigned it could take on 4,000 military, though in very tight quarters. During training at Camp Roberts, we had practiced jumping from a forty-foot tower into a large, deep-water pool. Now we understood what that maneuver was intended for: abandoning a ship in a fire or other disaster, in the high seas such as an enemy torpedo. It was crowded ship with not much room to move about, but we learned to get along.

Each soldier was assigned a place to sleep on a cot on a lower deck, in my case at the lowest level. To get there we had to descend several flights of stairs. The four cots were close together, a foot or so apart: one above the other. Once we settled into our cot it was difficult to try to climb out and go up to the main deck for a breath of fresh air. Shortly after sailing out of Seattle, I began to get seasick. My only recourse to keeping the malady from getting worse, was to force myself to erase it from my mind and think about fun things, my high school days as an example, or even thinking about a girl that seemed to be attracted to me during Elementary school years. It was, I thought, a mutual attraction and though it may seem odd, it worked. I got over my motion sickness. How Good God is to provide something to distract me from throwing up. My thoughts were about smiling at each other and during break we would seek each other out just to be near each other and that is about how far it went. We never saw one another again after the school year.

Aboard ship we were served two meals daily, morning and evening. The difficulty was that to obtain the first meal of the day, one had to rise early, about five or six in the morning to get in line and wait hours before finally entering the "Mess Hall," as it was metaphorically called. Our first experience in getting something to eat was a lesson in survival. After sitting down with our bowls of corn flakes, the ship swayed in the waves and our breakfasts went sliding down the table. Luckily, other men intercepted the wayward breakfasts and handed the bowls back in our direction. Had that not happened, we would have missed our first meal at sea. Everybody got a huge laugh. Once we had consumed the first serving of the day, we had to start lining up for supper. It takes time to feed 4,000 soldiers, and after each meal we had to return to the upper deck to form another line to come down again to the mess hall level for the evening meal.

That meant that we spent much of our time in line, not to miss out on a meal. I learned very quickly the meaning of "hurry up and wait." Most everybody passed the time playing cards, some even gambling their money away.

International Dateline

On the lighter side of this journey, we had an interesting experience, that of having to cross the International Dateline. It just so happened, that on this voyage we would lose out on one important day. Before crossing the dateline, it was the 24th of December, but when we passed to the other side, it was the 26th, so we missed Christmas Day. The Dateline is an imaginary line on the Ocean that changes the date when you go across the imaginary line. It is about longitude and latitude. It was a disappointment, but everyone took it in stride and celebrated the Birth of Our Lord anyway on the day after His birthday. The Navy personnel made a special meal for all. I had read about the Dateline in History Books, but to experience this imaginary line is a real experience. It is somewhere beyond the Hawaii Islands in the South Pacific.

The voyage from Seattle to our destination took 17 days. It was a miserable time for me, for I longed to get away from the metal and steel plating of the ship and feel solid ground under my feet again. But finally, after the long- and arduous-time aboard ship, we arrived at New Caledonia, a French island in the South Pacific, 750 miles east of Australia and 12,000 miles from Paris. The archipelago is part of the Melanesia sub-region.

The island was beautiful, even though I was not able to enjoy the sites very much. When I got off the ship the ground felt like it was waving up and down as my brain readjusted from 17 days of ocean motion. One of the good things that helped the adjustment was getting a Coca Cola drink which Salvation Army volunteers provided for us, although having to stand in line for an hour to get it. New Caledonia was truly an island paradise in the South Seas. We hated to leave it, but we were headed for battle.

TOKYO ROSE & CHARLIE

Chapter 13

On our first arrival on the island of Bougainville, within a safe perimeter secured by the Marines, to my surprise the first person I saw on the beach after exiting the land craft was Gil one of my friends from back home. I asked him "when did you get here?" and he said, "I've been here for two days." We spoke about our families back home and I went on my way. I never saw Gil again. I do not know what happened to him. He and his brothers were good friends of ours back home. Many of my friends joined the Army and Navy. One of my friends became a Paratrooper and fought in the Battle of the Bulge in Belgium where the Americans fought their way out of a trap surrounded by German Divisions.

We were deployed near the lines of battle, but in a safe area. One of the initial bits of conflict information we were given was to be on the alert for a lone Japanese plane that had been flying over every night to drop a single bomb on the troops. It was nerve-wracking to be watching out for this type of harassment. We came to call the plane and its pilot "washing machine Charlie," because the noise the aircraft made sounded exactly like a washing machine, and it came over our area at the same time each night. We were hungry for news from back home, but Toyo Rose interrupted the airways to peddle her propaganda. We could listen to the radio to try to obtain the latest news on the war and maybe some from home. But the only station we could tune in was one that featured the infamous Japanese propaganda peddler, "Tokyo Rose." This lady, with a very smooth and sexy voice and practically no trace of an Asian accent, made statements against American GIs that were blatantly false - or at the least, exaggerated - propaganda that she ballyhooed daily to destroy our morale…which of course, didn't work.

Presently we were briefed specifically on the true objective for which we were on Bougainville: Face-to-face combat with the Japanese. And so, began our foremost intention, to free the island from enemy control. And by the way, "washing machine Charlie" continued his nightly one-bomb blitzkrieg from that nauseatingly noisy airplane.

The White Sheets

One of the scariest things that took place when first arriving happened when we were gathered to begin our first combat with the enemy. Coming in the opposite direction from us were soldiers about one hundred yards away carrying loads in white sheets. I kept wondering what are they carrying? As they got nearer, I realized they were carrying their friends that had just been killed in battle wrapped in white sheets. I asked myself is that the way we are coming back. Since this was our first combat mission, I prayed for all of us.

A CRY FOR HELP

Chapter 14

Not long after we arrived on the island our company was given orders to engage the enemy and wrest control of area beyond our front lines. This was my first look beyond our front lines, and the area was a real war zone. From previous battles there were broken trees from artillery shells and holes from the blasts, jungle vines scattered all over. The area was totally devastated it looked like a strange land. The enemy began firing at us from many angles, and so we scattered in different directions firing back with our weapons. They came at us from hiding and the battle turned into chaos. I had no fear and jumped over broken logs and branches to see where the firing was coming from. This is what I trained for and put it to use. The noise from the battle was deafening – the noise the smoke the smell the yelling from both sides it was unbelievable the confusion of war. There were casualties on both sides. amid the battle a medic began crying for help to save a wounded soldier. "come and help me" I ran over to help. The soldier was bleeding from his arms and legs. I believe that a Japanese knee mortar had struck him, and he had wounds on his arms and legs. The medic cried out for someone to help him save this soldier. I ran to give him aid. He had to yell directions to me amid all the noise of the battle. He told me to apply pressure to his right arm to stop the bleeding while he gave him blood plasma to his left arm. I stopped the bleeding from his right arm, but the blood was squirting from his right leg, and his left leg was also bleeding. I had never seen blood squirting like that out of a human person and, it was awful at every heart beat the blood quirted. We did our best, but we could not save him. I felt so much empathy for the medic. For a moment of time, we shared love for our neighbor. We never encountered each other again. They are trained to save lives on the battlefield, but he was almost at the point of tears as his efforts to save a fellow soldier failed. What can I say about the soldier that died? He died defending his country and the people he loved. He was one of the dead soldiers that we brought back.

The soldier died in our arms. After the battle we carried our wounded to our front lines, but we could not bring back bodies of those who died, due to the raging battle. I saw one of our soldiers shoot an enemy soldier with the Garand rifle. It is so powerful that his head broke and rolled on the ground. When we got back to our safer area the Sargent Dave warned me not to act so cocky in battle, that I was endangering my life and that of others. He had seen me jumping over logs and firing at the enemy without concern for my safety. Later I will relate how this brave Sargent was severely wounded defending his country.

LOST IN THE JUNGLE

Chapter 15

I was a soldier in "F" Company of the 32nd Infantry of the Americal Division. I believe that it was also called the 37th Division. The Division had relieved a Marine Division. After having been in other battles on the island, I was assigned to go on patrol with five other soldiers to observe the enemy at night. We were to go into enemy lines and not engage them unless attacked. With me as first scout were First Lieutenant Gary, Sargent Dave, and three other soldiers the one I knew personally was Nathan.

It was my first time as a first scout. It is the job of the first scout to check the area before anyone else can proceed. It is a dangerous job because I was responsible for those coming after me. We left our main camp close to six o'clock in the evening. I would walk quietly about ten feet, through the thick jungle trail then motion the second scout to follow. And he would quietly motion to the others to follow. We did not speak it was only by hand signals that we communicated or whisper information if we had to. After a mile, we came to a river. I said to myself now what do we do.? The river was deep and turbulent, risky, and wide to cross but had a rope bridge that had been constructed I suppose by American engineers. The bridge resembled a miniature Golden Gate Bridge of San Francisco except that it was under water, about three or four feet under water. It had ropes along the river under water and tied to a tree on the other side of the river. It had other ropes supporting the bottom walkway and tied to the top ropes. If you can imagine the Golden Gate Bridge under a large river then you have an idea of how a marvel of engineering it was, but the bridge was not straight under the water it was semi-circular and went deeper into the water as one approached the center, and all hidden from the enemy. The towers of the Golden Gate bridge in San Francisco that are on each side of the shore of the sea support the cables. I remember going across the Golden Gate Bridge when I worked in Los Angeles for a Summer. I am not an engineer so that is the best I can explain the rope bridge.

I crossed the river first, and as I came to the middle of the river the water came up almost to my shoulders, so I carried my rifle with my arms extended as I walked across bridge. All of us were in full combat gear. It was scary it was a raging river deep and perilous.

Once across, I motioned to the second scout to proceed. His name was Bert. I could see he was nervous, but he got across and the rest followed one by one with the Lieutenant last. We talk as little as possible. We made signs with our hands. After another half mile, we came to what I thought would be a good place to observe the enemy. The area had been battered by artillery. There were fallen trees and holes everywhere. It looked like something from another planet it was so devastated.

I kept walking until I came to a denser area where we could hide from the enemy. I motioned to the officer, and he checked it out and thought it was alright. We separated from each other two by twos but not too far from each other. Now it was getting dark, and we settled in for what we thought would be an ideal place to keep a lookout for the enemy. We had no idea the enemy might be observing us, the night was eerie, and ghostly only the sounds of night creatures of the jungle could be heard. If you have ever camped out in the forest you know what I mean by creatures of the night, wolf cries, owls, etc.

About six o'clock in the morning chaos erupted. The Japanese started firing from their positions and began to fire at us with machine guns and mortars. They were firing from their hiding place, and we fired back. One of the mortars struck Sargent Dave and he was severely wounded.

BRAVERY UNDER FIRE

Chapter 16

The Lieutenant told me and my other companion Nathan to cover them while they built a stretcher out of branches to carry the injured man away. They worked quickly and used their shirts for support heedless of regard for their own safety. How they managed to build the gurney under fire is a great feat. Nathan and I kept firing at the enemy whether we killed any of them we do not know. The Lieutenant and three other soldiers left quickly with the wounded Sargent on a stretcher. My companion Nathan also took off after them leaving me alone to face the enemy. It was chaotic and anything can happen in a firefight. In training we were told do something even if it is wrong. The situation was urgent to get the wounded soldier to a hospital. He was hit from what I saw as a terrible devastating blow from a Japanese knee mortar. I was more frightened of mortars than bullets. The noise, plus concussion, could leave a person disabled and confused.

The enemy came in pursuit of me. I could hear them telling each other where I was in the dense jungle. I fired at them and ran into the jungle. They kept coming after me, but I eluded them I kept working my way through the thick trees and vines. At times I had to cut my way with my machete to clear a way. I ran into a wild boar and thought of killing it. We had been told that they were dangerous, but I would give my location, so I avoided the animal.

I must have cut my way through the thick jungle for hours

because it was getting late. I prayed that I would find the river. I knew that there was a volcano in the center of the island, but the jungle was so thick that I could not even see the sun. I finally came to an opening in the canopy of the trees and vines and saw the volcano in the distance. I knew that if I travelled away from the volcano, I would find the river.

I had started out about seven o'clock in the morning when I escaped from the enemy. It seemed like two o'clock in the afternoon. I kept checking the trees along the bank of the river to see if there was rope tied to it. I could not walk along the bank of the river except for a few feet at a time because of the huge bushes and vines. I would backtrack into the jungle and work my way back to the river and continue checking the trees for the bridge. It was a desperate situation if I did not find the river I would be lost in enemy territory. I thanked God when I found the tree with the ropes. It was now getting dark. I went across the bridge with the water up to my shoulders and carrying my rifle above my head. After crossing the river, I had to walk about a half- mile through enemy territory before arriving at the front lines where our area of safety was located.

I called out to the men that I was back, and they all came out in a hurry with their rifles ready to shoot. They thought it might be a trick from the enemy, but I kept yelling my name, and they asked for the password. I told them "Babe Ruth." The name "Babe Ruth" was the name of a famous baseball player. They called the officer before opening the gate, when he realized that I was the one who had been with him in the jungle earlier that day he ordered it to be opened.

They were all glad that I was back and had many questions of how I escaped from the enemy, and they said that I had been reported missing in action. Lost in the jungle with the enemy pursuing me is an ordeal I will never forget. I thank God and my guardian angel for their protection. I inquired about Sargent Dave who was gravely wounded and taken to a field hospital. but all they knew is that he was severely wounded. As I understand

Japanese mortars kill by concussion, and as I recall part of the back of the Sargent who was hit by the mortar was torn apart. His bravery and the brave soldiers who volunteered for the patrol received special medals in a ceremony which took place later, but the Sargent could not be with us. I have no idea if he lived through the ordeal.

MOONLIGHT ROSARY

Chapter 17

While in and near hostile territory, we had a barbed wire fence in front of our tents, with our foxholes by the side in case of an attack and the tents were spread about twenty feet apart. The length of the fence was about one -hundred yards and at one end was gate securely locked. There were two soldiers assigned to each area with a cot for each. The fences had booby traps attached. These deadly hazards were explosive hand grenades that were meant to be tripped by enemy fighters trying to cross through on suicide missions, no doubt, or just to kill Americans. Beyond the fence was enemy territory.

We took turns at night on guard duty, four hours on and four hours off. Early hours were when the adversary liked to attack, and we were always on edge anticipating their moves. I used to pray the Rosary at my time of rest or before sleeping while waiting to go on guard duty. At night, when it was not raining and the moonlight extremely bright, it almost seemed like midday. We had mosquito nets extended over our cots, to protect us from insect bites. One could easily see through the light fabric of the nets.

I was taken completely by surprise at one of our frequent meetings with Company officers, when First Lieutenant Cassidy told the men that "if they would pray as I did, things would get better for all.". He had seen me pray the Rosary in the bright moonlight. I truly believe that it was the Rosary that protected me from many dangers I faced in battle. There were other soldiers who were dedicated to prayer, and some were Catholic.

What is the rosary? It is a prayer using small beads strung together and we pray the Lord's Prayer (Our Father) on the large beads and the "Hail Mary" on the smaller ones. It has a crucifix or medal at the front, and it has a long tradition in the Church dating back centuries. It is a powerful weapon against evil spirits, but also for protection and petition in time of need. We as Catholics believe in Mary as the Mother of God because Jesus is God. He is true God and true man therefore: she is called Mother of God. As Catholics we pray for all people.

Time Out

During times of lull in the battle the Army promoted boxing matches between the different units to keep up morale in the troops. We had a few men from our unit that participated in these matches. They had preliminary bouts that led to a championship match between the two best contenders in each weight class. They had different weight classifications consequently at the end the best boxers met on a head-to-head bout. These were not casual matches. The different units were intent on their man winning it all. The troops attended every match and became familiar with the names of the contenders.

One of the best matches was between a Hispanic boxer from California and a Native American from one of our Western States. It was the final match of the event. The Native American took most of the rounds, but when it seemed that he was going to win it all the Spanish American came back strong in the final round and won the match. Not everyone was happy with the outcome, but all saw a terrific boxing match. It reminded me that we were against the ropes after being blasted at Pearl Harbor by the enemy losing 1,000 men and most of our battleships, but now we are coming back. It is possible in life to come back from what appears to be defeat as Our Lord Jesus did from the cross.

THE SIGN OF THE CROSS

Chapter 18

On a dark and cloudy day, we were sent on a reconnaissance patrol to explore the area of the jungle that we had not seen before. I was as usual the first scout leading the whole platoon of forty men into the jungle. We walked ten feet apart as usual, and it was my duty to check for snipers or any trouble ahead before the platoon could move on.

After about a half a mile I came to an open field. It was about seventy feet across to the other side, and to the South side of the field were what looked like mounds that indicated enemy bunkers. My thought was that the enemy had cleared this open space to create an open field of fire for their machine guns. I told my second scout, Raul, to relay this information to officer Cassidy in charge of the patrol. He gave the order for us to cross one by one over this open field. This seemed like a dangerous walk across, and I thought this might be the end of the line for me. I could see the scary look on Raul, he would be the second person to cross, as he was the second scout, and the officer had given orders to go across the seventy feet one by one when we are usually only ten feet apart.

Before crossing I made the sign of the cross. I needed heavenly protection and I prayed for it. I opened the trigger on my rifle gazing toward the dirt mounds or bunkers on the opposite side and began what seemed an eternity. I walked slow not to make any noise and made it to the other side of the open field. But I have never seen anyone as scared as Raul. Although I had been scared also. He had thick black hair and it was standing on end, but he too made it across, and the platoon began to cross.

As I continued, I spotted two Japanese sitting against a tree. I was about to shoot them when I realized they were dead evidently killed by a bombardment because their faces were bloody with a stare of the dead. We did not encounter the enemy on this patrol, but we learned they were not in this area of the jungle perhaps because of the artillery bombardment that had occurred days before. The Sign of the Cross for Catholics is a sign of our baptism and recalls for us the cross of Christ.

THE LONELY ROAD

Chapter 19

Sometime later, after experiences in battle, our Company was ordered to go out once again to engage the enemy. Headquarters was expecting a large attack from the enemy coming from the north end of the island and we were to engage them. We departed in full combat gear prepared for battle. A U.S. Army Company is made up of four platoons of forty men each, plus a heavy weapons Company and a few officers under the direction of a Company Commander.

As First Scout it was my duty to lead the way through the jungle trail and we had to cross the rope bridge again that was inside enemy territory. As I walked for several hundred yards, suddenly to my surprise, I came upon a road in the jungle, and I do not know who constructed the road. It was a well - constructed road. There was no activity on the road it seemed like a very lonely road. I told my second scout to relay the information to the captain that there was a road ahead. Since the rest of the Company was still in the jungle area and could not see further then the soldier ahead. The order came back to check any huts or enemy bunkers. My specific orders were to move forward cautiously in to check both sides of the road. Though careful, I was very tense not knowing if my next move would be my last. I was responsible for 200 men behind me in the jungle a column of human beings that stretched a good way back through the jungle and the only soldier I could see is my Second Scout, and as I named him before his name was Bert.

As was the custom, we quietly advanced in single file, ten feet apart to prevent heavy casualties in an unexpected ambush. I could not see any of those behind me except for the Second Scout who stayed on the road while I checked any enemy huts, or campsites or areas of concern where danger might lurk. I came upon three enemy soldiers about a hundred yards away. They spotted me at the same time I saw them. I hit the ground with my rifle ready. I saw them run into the jungle. Soon I came upon a hut on the side of the road. I immediately informed the second Scout, and he relayed the message to the Commander by passing the word back. He ordered that no one move forward until I gave the signal to proceed.

Everything was quiet and I walked very slowly with my finger on the rifle trigger, as I entered the area where the hut was a Japanese soldier was lying on a wooden bench with his back to me. He was to my left as I entered and he looked back, saw me, and tried to stand up from the bunk but I shot him. Then I heard voices emanating from a pillbox to my right. I grabbed a hand grenade and pulled the pin forgetting to hold the safety handle, so the grenade was ready to explode within 10 seconds. In a moment of panic, I tossed it with strong force into the underground pillbox while, at the same time, diving behind a log. It was the log that saved me.

After the explosion all was quiet, I was not injured, so I assumed the grenade had done its job. I got up to check the pillbox and saw no signs of life but noticed that my rifle had been badly damaged by the explosion. I threw the grenade with such force that unknowingly my rifle fell near the enemy pillbox. That made me realize how lucky I was to get behind that log. The rifle had suffered a bent barrel and was no longer of any use. I suddenly knew that when I tossed the grenade with my right arm the rifle had gone with it. I reported to the Second Scout what had happened. He in turn, relayed the message back. He then told me the Commander had asked to see me. After relating the whole episode to him, he gave me another rifle that had belonged to the radio man and ordered me to proceed with the mission. It seemed he was satisfied with the results. It was strange that he did not send other soldiers to check and see if there were other Japanese in the area. He was anxious to proceed with the mission.

That anguishing skirmish stuck in my mind for a long time, the fact that I participated in the deaths of other human beings. Yes, we were fighting for our country, but the truth be told it was a matter of "kill or be killed." I assumed that the soldiers in the pillbox had been killed by the hand grenade.

We continued advancing on that desolate road until dusk and came across those same three Japanese soldiers I had seen earlier. They were killed by our men as they were cooking rice. That mission ended with no other enemy encounters. Who had built that road? I do not know, but it was a long and lonely road.

DEATH ON THE MOUNTAIN

Chapter 20

On another Patrol we had been walking through the jungle all day and came upon a high mountain. It was getting late by the time we got to the top. Everyone was tired and hungry. We came under fire by a sniper when digging our foxholes for the night. By the time most had finished it was dark. Our foxholes were about six feet apart. Evidently one of the soldiers had left the group without telling anyone and was hit by a sniper. By his voice I could tell he was about ten yards away from the group and kept calling for help. I thought the medics would go out to give some aid. Most everyone heard him calling out, but the order was that no one must leave their post after dark. He kept calling in pain.

Something was wrong and he could not get back by himself. It was heart rending, and most everyone heard him but made no attempt to go out in the dark to help him, for it could possibly be an enemy soldier impersonating an American to kill him. We had been warned of such incidents at training. After a long while the painful crying for help stopped. In the early morning several of us went out to see what had happened. Leaning by a tree was a young soldier whom I knew with his head against a tree. He was dead. It seemed like he had been praying to God in his last moments. He had been shot in the leg and he bled to death: Death on a mountain far away from home. My conscience still bothers me today. Why did I not go out to help him? It speaks volumes about the tragedy of war. We resumed on patrol for several days, but we did not encounter any more of the enemy, so we returned to our camp.

A Day Off to Relax

Once on a day off, Lugo and I went off not what we thought was a safe part of the jungle. Lugo was from Corpus Christi, Texas. He was stocky and a strong swimmer. We came upon a lagoon. Since it was a hot day of about 120 degrees he decided to go for a swim. I could not bring myself to jump into the water fearing that there were water snakes or some other creatures lurking, but as it turned out he had a good swim and we returned to base. Some of the soldiers were at the beach swimming in the ocean and curious about several two-hundred- pound turtles that came out of the ocean and crawled around the area. There were two men who were excellent swimmers. They would swim to a small island about a mile away. It was not occupied so they were free to spend time and then swim back.

It was at this time that our platoon officer Cassidy told me that he would like to see me attend Officers Candidate School. He asked me to write a letter to my family back home. I believe that he wanted to see if I could speak and write well, but I never wrote the letter we were sent out on a combat mission, and we never talked about it again. This officer by the name Cassidy is the one who had seen me praying the rosary in the moonlight. He was tall and lean, and he was a good officer.

THE CRYING SOLDIER

Chapter 21

We left early one morning on a patrol again we were only six persons on this patrol. Lieutenant Gregg, and five enlisted men. I was the first scout, and after going about a half a mile through the jungle we came upon a large body of water. It was almost like a lagoon or a small lake, and there was no other way to go because of the jungle vines and dense vegetation all around. Lieutenant Gregg told me to go across. I was concerned and hesitant afraid of snakes or other reptiles that might be in this body of water. I lifted my rifle and began to cross. The water came up to my waist and I got across. It must have been about eighty feet across, and the officer, and four men came right behind him they got across except Jeff.

He would not cross he was crying as he stood facing the lagoon-like lake and seeing us on the other side. He was on the other staring at us. It was up to the officer to decide what to do, and he tried to encourage him to cross, but he would not do so. We could not leave him alone in the jungle. Finally, Lieutenant Gregg, who was about six feet tall and strong went back across the water and carried him on his shoulders. Jeff was about five feet four inches tall and perhaps that is why he was afraid to cross. Our Lieutenant was as brave as they come. I believe their training at Boot Camp pays off in acts of bravery.

It is not only the crossing but being exposed to the wet clothes all over again. In the jungle the heat of your body dries your clothes. On this patrol we did not encounter the enemy, but we found another way to get back to camp and reported that no enemy was encountered.

THE 30 DAY MISSION

Chapter 22

One day word came down from headquarters to prepare for a thirty-day mission into enemy territory. When the day came, we set out with our fulfilled packs and those things necessary for such a long period out in the jungle.

It was a trek in the jungle by the whole Battalion. A battalion is a military unit made up of a headquarters company and four infantry companies. The artillery unit was not with us. A Catholic Chaplain Father O'Connell was with us. When the time came, we were all lined up in single file. It was a long line of soldiers going into battle to engage the enemy. We did not know what to expect. This was not something done in haste. It had been planned for some time as the word was that a big offensive was underway by the Japanese to attack our forces.

We set out in single file along the trail about six o'clock in the evening and were told to pick a little flower from the field. It was a small flower that lights up in the dark and to place it in the back of our backpack so that in the dark we could follow one another into the jungle, and it seemed like a great idea. Everyone put the small flower on their backpack and things went smoothly following one another as it began to get dark. As usual we must stay about ten feet behind the soldier in front to avoid heavy casualties in case of attack.

But the strangest thing happened as we went along the trail in the dark, we came upon a field that was full of these small flowers which light up in the dark. The troops began to go in different directions according to where they thought was the soldier in front. This went on for several hours until the whole Battalion was scattered. It was about ten o'clock at night when word came down to bed down wherever we were until daylight. It was chaotic but I believe we all got a little sleep.

In the morning we regrouped and continued our mission. It was slow moving through the jungle with so many troops. I cannot remember which day we ran into the enemy, but they were on top of the hill, and we began to fight our way up. It was late in the evening by the time we took the hill and captured three Japanese soldiers. We did not suffer any casualties.

We dug our foxholes and prepared for the night. When we woke up in the morning, we were told something very terrible. The three Japanese soldiers who had been captured were found dead. How this happened we were not told.

As we continued our mission the rain came and made it very miserable. The food that was supposed to be dropped for us from an airplane was dropped in the wrong location, so we never got it. We existed on our canned rations which we carried with us. Our canned rations consisted of hash browns, meat and beans and other canned goods. After a while the canned food is tasteless. But what do you expect in war?

As the days went on, we got caught in a bombardment. The enemy became aware of our presence and shelled us with artillery. I remembered seeing our Chaplain, a Catholic priest running for cover. I jumped into a big hole where there were several dead bodies. I could not tell if they were dead American soldiers or enemy.

When the bombardment stopped, we continued our mission. But the rain kept on coming and going up a steep hill we kept sliding down due to the rain making the climb slippery. We finally made it to the top of the hill and as it was getting late, we began to dig our foxholes for the night.

It was on the top of this hill that I had one of the most amazing experiences of my life. As I had finished digging my foxhole for the night and I was crawling into it I dropped my prayer book that I carried with me. It was a prayer book that sister Rosita had given me when I was at Saint Anthony's Orphanage as a child of seven years old. Out of the prayer book fell a holy picture of Mary the Virgin Mother of God. At the time that I received the picture from Sister Rosita, I did not like it, I wanted a picture of the Sacred Heart of Jesus, but I did not get one. Even though I had this picture of Mary for many years I had not taken notice of it until this day in the jungle. It had a blue ribbon around it, and I never saw anything so beautiful as this picture of Mary in a jungle far away from home. I felt that God was speaking to me that night, and I prayed to Him and said are you going to let me die here without receiving you again in Holy Communion? Thirty days gone from our base camp with the same clothes and the same food, but we completed our mission without meeting a large force of the enemy.

Upon our return, Father O'Connel said Mass on the hood of a jeep. He put a blanket over the hood, and placed the chalice upon it. I thought he would speak of the hardships endured in the jungle. But he spoke of the souls in Purgatory. It was a pleasant surprise. They suffer more than we do here on earth.

Kelli MacPhail Gómez; Minnie P. Dávila; Brooklyn Resecker

SQUAD LEADER

Chapter 23

I was named a Squad Leader after some time as a First Scout. As a Squad Leader I was elevated to the rank of Sargent, and I oversaw twelve soldiers. We went on a mission with the Lieutenant to try and recover the name tags of soldiers who had been killed previously.

After going through the jungle for about a mile we came under machine gun fire. We got pinned down and could not move. I felt the bullets whistling next to my head, so I put my head down. It got so bad that the officer in charge told everyone to get out as best we could. We could not see where the firing was coming from because the Japanese built bunkers under the ground and then planted bushes and other foliage to prevent detection. We had to crawl on the ground to avoid being hit. We did as the officer said and returned to our camp and we would search for the dog tags later. Everyone got back to camp safely, but it was a harrowing experience being pinned down by machine gun fire, but we had practiced that while in Boot Camp that is crawling on our bellies to prevent being hit, but in this area, we could not move toward the enemy to engage them as we were prevented by jungle trees and vines.

<u>The Nightmare</u>

When I first went into war, I was a bit careless, but now that I have seen what war really is and what it does to the mind from all the noise the sight of death and wounded soldiers, I began to worry about my chances of ever getting out alive, perhaps my faith was not as strong as I thought, or my courage was lessening.

One night, after my watch, I fell into a deep sleep, but was suddenly awakened by a noise and rose at once. My first thought was that it was time for me to go back on duty, but instead I saw a person coming towards me. I grabbed my rifle and was about to shoot when the image coming toward me called my name. It turned out to be William the soldier who slept in the cot next to me, and we took turns for guard duty. I would have shot him if he had not called out my name. William was a lanky Texan who was always complaining about "my aching back", but he was brave soldier unafraid and always tossing out remarks about the Toughness of life. He was a happy man but was not afraid to do battle with the enemy. He was designated to carry the Browning Automatic rifle in our squad. The rest of us carried the Garand rifle and the officer carried their smaller rifle. This would have been a tragedy due to my lack of sleep and intense stress; this stressful period made me weaker, and a far cry from when I had first arrived to go into battle with a "gung-ho" attitude. I will relate later some soldiers who could not cope with the shock of war.

RECRUITS AND MENTAL CASES

Chapter 24

The new recruits had just come from the states and were eager to meet new soldiers and help with the battle against the enemy. These two recruits that I had brought from my meeting with the Colonel who received the soldier who was mentally sick. They spent the afternoon getting acquainted and sharing with us about things back home.

They were assigned to the bunker next to me and my companion William. The Japanese were aware of our positions that were protected by barbed wire and hidden grenades. They did not try to enter our area but with rapid gunfire and knee mortars would cause casualties among our troops. They would always attack around four o'clock in the morning.

We fired back from positions not knowing if we inflicted casualties on them. But this one night from our bunker we heard a booming noise from the next bunker. Investigating in the morning we found our two new recruits dead in their bunker. As I understand knee mortars kill by concussion and inflict severe injuries and death by the horrible noise. The recruits were younger than us and very happy to be in combat, but their end came suddenly.

Jesus tells us in the Gospel we do not know the day or the hour when we will die, but he warns us to prepare for our death. In war we prepare by prayer.

I will later relate how one recruit who came to us two weeks before the war ended was killed by a sniper. What a mystery: I had been in the war for over a year in the thick of battle, and these brave friends died within a few weeks. We pray for them.

Mental Dilemma

There were many brave soldiers in my Company "F", but as the war dragged on there were a few who gave up. I recall this one, he was a big and strong soldier around five-feet-ten and muscular like a weightlifter. He was not with us on arrival but joined us later as a recruit. Coming from battle one day, he suddenly stopped talking to anyone. He was in the thick of battle, perhaps his childhood had something to do with it. He would spontaneously break out crying and it made us all wonder if he was really fit for combat. He would not eat but avoided us. The officer in command tried to reason with him, but to no avail. It is a pitiful sight to see this happen to anyone, let alone a fighting man. We trained for many months to fight a war and then to see someone give up shakes the very foundations that been established in our training. Some felt it was a bad example for others. After many avenues taken to try to help this fellow, he was finally sent for medical psychiatric evaluation.

There was a story circulating in the Army that the best way to be sent back home was to shoot yourself in the foot. I never saw any of that, but there was also the case of the young soldier who everyone looked up to. He was a born leader put in charge of a squad, that is, a twelve-man unit. He was also big and strong not very tall but of medium height with a pleasant personality. He looked like a movie star. He had been with us on several missions. As time went on, he too succumbed to the ordeals of war. With seemingly involuntary bouts of crying, he stopped talking just as the first man. Every one of us became concerned, wondering how this could happen to a good soldier who appeared to be full of energy, projecting a good future. What goes on in the mind of men in battle, as far as I knew, had not been fully evaluated or even considered enough as a major problem. Most of us were simply in the dark about these psychological flash points. If studies have been made, they need to be reviewed. It seems.

One day I was assigned the task of taking this soldier because he was being a bad influence on the rest of the Company. I was to take him to headquarters, which was about a mile away from our camp along a narrow trail in the jungle. He kept tripping over his feet and crying as we went along. It even entered my mind that this soldier might be feigning a medical condition just to be sent home. I wondered myself if I might pretend that I was sick and could be sent home as well. But it was just my imagination running away with me since I could never really see myself doing such a thing. My faith in God was with me since my childhood which I had learned from the Nuns at Saint Anthony's.

When we arrived at our destination, the person in charge was a Colonel. He was surrounded by a group of soldiers under his command. A colonel is a high-ranking officer in the Armed Forces. He asked the soldier I brought to him what his purpose was in coming to see him. The troubled fellow said nothing, he just kept crying, and would lie on the ground. Then the Colonel realized why he had been sent to him. He roughed the soldier up, and I have never seen anyone so angry. He cursed him in front of the other soldiers, and I imagine they were scandalized by the way the Colonel treated the man, as I recall he even kicked him. I believe he was put in a hospital and sent home. The Colonel then turned to me and asked what I was doing at headquarters. I answered that I had been put in charge of delivering the man to him and, I was told to pick up two new recruits who had been assigned to our Company. He directed some of his own men to bring the two rookies, who I then escorted back to my Company.

In reflecting on the actions of the Colonel, I pondered whether it was right or wrong, as he seemed insensitive to the man's problem. For me, there was no easy answer. He had his job, but he could have had more restraint and, it was apparently difficult to deal with a soldier who, as I said, had given up. Combat seemed to have broken the man's spirit. I felt that in weak moments, the same could have happened to me. Thank God that He had given me faith to endure in time of trial, be they by war with visible enemies or with combating the devil in the spiritual realm. I say this because my life of prayer at an early age, has given me my faith in God. I hope that the men who were sent back received the help that they needed for who am I to judge anyone. "Who are you to judge your neighbor?[11]

DEATH IN A FOXHOLE

Chapter 25

As already related, I was appointed First Scout in Company F and served in that position for a good while, after which I was named Squad Leader and elevated to the rank of Sergeant, thus putting me in charge of 12 men.

One of the members of my unit named Sam made it known that he should be Squad Leader; he felt he was more capable than I to lead the group. He got his chance one day when he reported untruthfully to the officer in charge that I had allowed members of my unit to play cards while on duty. It was a bum rap because I had not given any such permission; they simply did it on their own and the officer believed Sam. So, I lost my job in leading the squad.

Afterward, in another fire fight with Japanese we were ordered to take the hill where we were receiving fire. We began by firing mortar fire and then shooting our way up. The Lieutenant gave the order to dig foxholes right at our current positions since it was getting dark This required the Squad Leader to be at the head of the unit, closest to the top of the hill. We did as we were ordered and spent a very dark and scary night in our foxholes. Sam our new Squad Leader was in the foxhole closest to the enemy. Just before daylight, there was noise and commotion near the top of the hill. we heard a loud explosion in the vicinity of the most forward foxhole where Sam was. Then silence.

As the sun came up, we learned that a Japanese soldier had

crawled into the foxhole where Sam the Squad Leader occupied. Did he stick a knife into Sam? A struggle ensued, a hand grenade detonated, and both were killed.

I have often thought about this incident because I believe that Sam had given his life for his country…. but also, in a somewhat human way, for me. I should have been in that foxhole had I remained Squad Leader. I have often prayed for Sam's immortal soul. Later that same day we were able to take the hill and killed the enemy soldiers.

The Gentle Soldier

I had another Mid-Westerner friend, one named Alex. He was of average height and a very calm disposition. By external appearances he did not fit the mold of a daring Commando or someone who would harm another. Yet, he had to carry a rifle like the rest of us, as well as hand grenades and a belt of bullets. In my combat experiences, I came to genuinely believe that many soldiers were only plain guys from ordinary families, hard workers who were drafted and pulled away from their comfortable environments and brought to a far-off land to fight in a war they knew very little about.

It was the tough training that turned these mostly young, inexperienced lads into fighting machines. Most of them did not fit into the movie-hero types but were genuinely disposed to lay down their lives for their country. Rough, tough, calm, gentle giants, all fighting together for a common cause.

Alex and I talked quite often about religion and things of God. He was not Catholic but dedicated to his Christian faith. He loved to sing religious songs and hymns. As the war progressed, I lost track of Alex, and I never saw him again. I hope he made it back home in good health.

There was another soldier named Ned who kept singing:

"What a beautiful place must be heaven,

what a beautiful place that must be,

*I'm going to spend my vacation in heaven,
with all the angels and saints…(Author unknown)*

THE GRASSY HILL

Chapter 26

On another day we were chasing a few enemy soldiers up a grassy hill, while at the same time firing at them. They did not fire back they kept running up the grassy hill. It was here that one of them who had been hit, but still alive, was finished off by one of our men with his rifle butt. Other Japanese combatants also died in that skirmish. When it was over, some of our troops took the wrist watches, rifles, swords from the dead soldiers plus other items. I was reluctant to take anything because it did not seem right. Later our Commander ordered all those items of war to be turned in for storage. Later, a Lieutenant, two other soldiers and I, whose actions had been crucial to the rescue of that wounded soldier written about in "Lost in the Jungle" chapter, could take whatever we wanted from the stored cache of arms and other captured combat paraphernalia. I chose a sword and rifle which I brought home after the war.

At a parade later, the Lieutenant was awarded the Silver Star for his bravery in the rescue. The other two soldiers and I received the Bronze Star. As mentioned in my preamble: The Bronze Star is a decoration awarded to members of the U.S. Armed Forces for: "Heroic achievement, heroic service, meritorious achievement, meritorious service in a combat zone." This final story ends the Bougainville campaign for our unit. Now we move on to other Campaigns.

THE LEYTE CAMPAIGN

Chapter 27

From Bougainville 132nd. Regiment of the Americal (aka:23rd. Division) invaded Leyte, landing onshore October 1944. It is one of the Philippines' largest islands, seventh in land mass, situated Southeast of Luzon, 121 miles long and very mountainous with beautiful valleys, tall palm trees and wildly matted jungles. Leyte is also famous for General Douglas MacArthur's well celebrated return to the Philippines, as he had promised when forced to leave earlier when many American Soldiers who had been captured by the Japanese were forced to walk for many miles to a prisoner's camp. Many of the soldiers died on the road and were abandoned. A trek now known as "The Bataan Death March."

Snake In the Grass

Japanese fighters had occupied Leyte since the beginning of the war, and they were firmly entrenched when the U.S. arrived. Our first night was hectic, especially with so many troops, tanks and other supporting heavy equipment being unloaded on the beaches. With full gear we went to our assigned areas and bedded down on the ground covered by our ponchos in case it rained. The enemy was nearby, suddenly, from seemingly out of nowhere, a large snake, like a python, crawled over three of us who were bedded down close to each other, and crawled into the bushes. From that moment on we had difficulty falling asleep because we thought it might return.

FIERCE COMBAT

Chapter 28

The next morning, we began our long-awaited battle and prepared for combat on Leyte. It was a search for Japanese installations. My orders were to carry the radio and walk aside the- the- newly assigned officer. His name was Lieutenant Jerry. The radio was for crucial communications with artillery and air support units that we might need their assistance. From our vantage point we spotted Japanese combatants in a valley below. They were loading equipment into trucks. The Lieutenant called on the radio for artillery. The "big guns" responded with shell fire aimed at the coordinates we provided. After the shelling, many of the enemy took off. Our infantry pursued the enemy soldiers toward a hill. They opted not to engage us, instead began running up the hill. We were able to kill them.

A short while later, patrolling the area, we were fired upon from a hill. The Officer leader ordered all to charge up the steep hill covered with small trees and bushes. It was treacherous and the enemy was looking down at us. I was by the side of Lieutenant Jerry carrying the radio, as the conflict intensified on both sides. The bullets whizzing by and mortar fire coming down made it difficult for us to return fire, we returned sporadic fire to help contain our ground. Some of the soldiers began retreating, running down the hill. To stem the sudden pullback officer Jerry drew his 45-caliber pistol and ordered them back or he would shoot them. He yelled at the top of his voice, and he meant to shoot. Fortunately, the soldiers obeyed, returning fire as we all climbed to higher ground. With superior power and tossing grenades up the hill we took the hill with the enemy suffering heavy casualties. We killed several soldiers on top of the hill. I admired Officer Jerry, He was tall and maybe a little overweight and walked kind of slow, but he stood up during enemy fire, and ordered the men to return to battle. I stood with him for I carried the radio alongside. We were not trained to run away or retreat from battle, but the danger of being killed going up a steep hill with the enemy firing down can be intimidating, but their courage revived, and the battle was won. I thank God that my faith in him carried me to be brave, and to give an example to the lieutenant that I was with him no matter the outcome would be.

On another day we went into an area surrounded by cocoanut trees along with jungle-type greenery, we covered several miles experiencing no resistance. On this patrol, I was designated to cover the rear of the column, since I had experience as scout. Observing our previous policy of staying ten feet apart to avoid casualties. Unexpectedly, a sniper shot one of our men when we were returning from the patrol. He died on the spot. We attempted to pursue the sniper, but he evaded us and disappeared. It was a long difficult patrol with no rest.

Bringing up the end of the column was difficult for me. I began to feel extremely weak and at one final point, could go no further. I lay down beside a coconut tree, rested and began to recover. I even tried to knock down a coconut from a tree but failed. With great effort I was able to stand up and start walking to join my platoon, which was now a half mile ahead. It was a risky and lonely trek, but finally successful in rejoining my companions. The real tragedy for this patrol was that the soldier who was killed by the sniper had been with our Company only two weeks. He had come directly from the states to fight for his country. The war ended two weeks later, but he could not be with us. His name was Ben. The end of that battle on Leyte led to the next beachhead, but without me.

A TROPICAL ILLNESS

Chapter 29

While on Leyte, I became ill with recurring Malaria, I had had it before on Bougainville also with Hookworm, and a terrible earache caught on an Island while swimming in a lake. The medics could not diagnose out what my disease was because Malaria does not repeat itself so quickly, so they said. I was transported by a transport plane to an Army Hospital on the island. During 45 days of recovery, my unit had to prepare for its next assignment. And that task would be making a beachhead on the Island of Cebu. While I was at the hospital the nurses were kind and the doctors were excellent. The best thing was the food was fresh and tasty. I was able to attend some movies in an outdoor setting when my health improved. Some entertainers from the States came to provide some smiles on our faces, and it was something the troops enjoyed.

Upon release from the hospital, my orders were to re-join my Company. At that time, the only way to get to my Company was aboard a Navy Destroyer. Headquarters made plans for me to get on board and head for my destination which happened to be headed in the same direction which was Cebu Island where the battle was raging. I believe the destroyer was on the way to help with the bombardment of the Island. I was the only soldier on the ship and, was assigned a berth on a lower deck. The sailors I met were kind to me.

I had never been on a large fighting ship like a destroyer and as I rested in my bunk, I began to get seasick. Outside the seas had suddenly turned stormy and was raining. To relieve my misery, I went up top looking for some fresh air. There were no sailors around, and the turbulent sea made my motion nausea even worse. I did not realize how dangerous the deck was with the ocean in such agitation. I had a precarious moment when I slipped on the wet deck as the ship swayed in the storm. I slid around and had it not been for my being able to grab on to a railing, I would have been tossed overboard. No one would have known what happened to me. I did get some fresh air and felt better. I was kind of lonely all alone in the lower deck and wondering how long the trip would last.

BATTLE OF CEBU- GOSHEN HILL

Chapter 30

It was not a long voyage from the Island of Leyte to Cebu. The invasion had already begun when I got off the ship. I left the destroyer and was surprised by the chaotic situation. The Americal Division (aka: 23rd. Division) along with supporting units were in place, already in combat with the Japanese forces.

The enemy controlled the top of a high mountain called Goshen Hill and were firing their twenty Millimeter bullets and mortars down on our troops, whose mission it was for us to wrest hold of the mountain from them. The mountain reminded me of the Sandia Mountains in New Mexico It was a difficult picture to witness because the enemy had the advantage. The sound of cannon fire, explosions and thick, black smoke were all around the ravaged city. Meanwhile supplies, including heavy equipment, were being unloaded along a nearby beachhead while other U.S. Army units were setting up to support the troops on the ground.

I reported to Quartermaster Supply to be issued a rifle and other gear required for combat and went on my way in search of the Company "F" companions. I asked everywhere, but all I got was "they're somewhere on the mountain." I had no alternative but to start upward. I remember thinking that it was like climbing 10,000-foot Sandia Mountain back home in Albuquerque, but the mountain on Cebu was not that high. On the way up shells were exploding, and the noise was deafening. A mortar shell landed nearby which stunned me and other soldiers also making their way up. We all hit the ground attempting to avoid being injured or killed. The jarring I got from the explosion caused me to start bleeding from my eyes and ears. I had to wipe the blood with my shirt. Not knowing if the injury was serious, I was more careful climbing the mountain.

Recovering my senses, I was able to make it to the battle front. I continued to inquire about the whereabouts of Company "F," but the responses were: "keep climbing." So, I did, and miraculously was finally able to locate my unit. I was told to continue uphill, and to fire on what appeared to be enemy bunkers from where the fire was coming. With combat superiority we were soon able to take the mountain from the Japanese in a few days. It had taken several days but not without casualties…. on both sides. I heard later that we lost four- hundred soldiers. When the fighting ended, I went to the medic station to report my bleeding eyes and ears I figured that I needed medication. I was bewildered to hear one of the medics say: "Don't worry about it. We are not going to give you a Purple Heart; your injury is not serious; it should go away." The Purple Heart is a medal given to those who suffer serious wounds in battle, but winning one was not my intention, just simply thought I needed medical attention. I accepted what I was told as treating the injury lightly, surmising that the medic knew better than I. The battle for Goshen Hill was a fierce combat battle and four hundred and ten American soldiers were killed. Since I was part of that battle, I will never forget Goshen Hill. As I understand the Goshen family still owns Goshen Hill.

SAD NEWS FROM HOME

Chapter 31

After the American forces conquered the island, we were given a rest period. It was during that respite that I got an order to report to the Chaplain, that he had something to tell me. Arriving at his tent he told me to sit down. I had no idea what this face-to-face with a priest meant. He handed me a telegram that was thirty days old. I was astounded to learn its contents; it informed me that my older brother Arthur had died back home of a heart attack in New Mexico. He was about 27 years old when he died. I wept bitterly for my brother Arthur, yes, he had a speech impediment and people made fun of him, but he was a very loving person. I know that God has a special place for him in heaven.

Arthur had a lifetime speech impediment and as a result was declared 4-F, a classification that denied him entry into service in the military. His dream had been to join in the war effort but could not. The Chaplain was kind and understanding and told me that he would offer prayers for Arthur's soul. I was quite saddened by my brother's death and concerned for my mother's well-being during this time; worried that I could offer no assurances that I would ever rejoin my family, and that my mom might lose another son, but this time in war.

I also received in the mail a copy from my mom of an article that appeared in the Albuquerque newspaper, "Albuquerque soldier lost in action." This referred to my being lost in the jungle. She wrote that the family thought I had been killed in action. I wrote to her to let them know that I was ok.

During a rest period on Cebu, I met a girl by the name of Sally. We talked about our families and how they had suffered under the Japanese occupation. I shared some of my candies and cigarettes with her family, something most of the soldiers did for other families on Cebu. I did not smoke while in the army. They were very thankful. We promised each other that we would keep in touch by mail. I did write to her when I was back in the states. I did receive one letter from her, but that was the last time I heard from her.

The Battle of Cebu was the last of my combat experiences. I thank God for allowing me the privilege of helping defend my country against the tyranny of other nations and that his protective hand was always there in all the dangerous tests and ordeals. He gave my fellow soldiers and me to endure the dangers of battle constantly under His loving care.

A STRANGE COUNTRY

Chapter 32

While sporadic fighting on Leyte and Cebu, my Company was put on alert that an officer from Headquarters was on the way. When he arrived, we were ordered to "fall in," which meant the whole unit had to line up in formation. We sensed that something especially important was about to take place.

The officer announced: "We need volunteers for a special mission. It will be a great undertaking, an honor for those who choose to become part of it." He invited any interested soldier to step forward. At that very moment I was ready to volunteer, but something inside made me think twice. As I recall, only two or three took the leap, one being from my squad. He was a good friend named Johnny from Roswell in my home state, and obviously very brave. Later, when the war was over, I read in a local newspaper that he had been with the first troops to engage in combat in the Korean War and had been killed during one of the major conflicts. I felt a great loss for we had been through many battles together. Sometimes we need to have prudence to avoid being drawn into other conflicts that spring up in other parts of the world when the person may have done enough in serving our country in the battles already fought.

When word came that the Japanese had surrendered; we were all celebrating, cheering, and giving Victory signs to everyone we met. Our unit was immediately ordered to get ready to go to Japan. we had to move quickly. Soon a ship came and loaded us on board. We sailed across the Western Pacific, destination: the port of Yokohama, Japan. The ocean was stormy and cold, for it was almost winter in the Far East.

Upon landing we were driven by trucks to our designated station. It was a long trip, none of us knowing what to expect. We arrived in the late evening at a town called Hiratsuka, Southwest of Tokyo. We were part of one of the first contingents of U.S. Army troops to arrive in the defeated country. We were sent to guard an ammunition dump near Hiroshima. We had heard that the first Atomic Bomb had devastated this large city, but had no idea how many casualties had resulted, nor about the lingering effects a nuclear weapon would bring. Later it was reported that more than a quarter-million had died, just in the Hiroshima blast.

Our Company was quartered in Japanese barracks which were very cold with no heating systems. The assignment was quite scary, guard duty in a foreign country and in such large warehouses. We took turns during the night to surveil the area with our weapons ready in case of trouble. I only remember how cold and dark Japan was. After my first stint on guard, I experienced something very stunning. It was early morning and as the sun arose, I was struck by a beautiful mountain in the distance. The beautiful mountain was snow-covered and very majestic.

During this assignment we were forced to take cold showers because there was no hot water available, the showers were outside the barracks and in the cold Japanese Winter you had to hurry or freeze. As time went on and we became fixtures to the local population, we realized that the native citizens were not looking for trouble. They just stared, and we stared right back, never abandoning our rifles, wherever we happened to encounter them. We were not allowed to visit Hiroshima or go anywhere near it.

There were later times in which we could go sightseeing without weapons. A buddy and I even went to Tokyo once.

Dialogue between the Japanese citizenry and their conquerors began to develop, and many relations turned friendly. Tokyo, in those days, was one the largest cities in the world with many interesting sights and lots to buy, such as souvenirs to take home.

After a few months of duty in Japan I was sent home. The voyage home on the ship was cold and the weather stormy, but what I remember most fondly of my stay there is that big, beautiful, majestic mountain near Hiroshima. What a tragedy, I thought, how such a treasure is often ignored and taken for granted. Each time I looked at it I reminisced about my own hometown of Albuquerque and likewise the beautiful, majestic Sandia mountains. The name "sandia" in Spanish means "watermelon," because each sunset, most of the year turns it red. In the winter it is often snow-covered just like the ones I enjoyed gazing at in Japan. The name Hiroshima may have been changed after the War.

I also recall how thankful I am to God for His protection for my fellow-soldiers and me all during the war and especially from any radiation sickness. The first Atomic Bomb was dropped, causing heartache and devastation for so many of God's Japanese children.

A SOLDIER RETURNS HOME

Chapter 33

Returning home from the war and reuniting with my family, they were so happy to see me, and I began visiting relatives and having a good time. I even went to a wedding of one of my cousins and drank too much and I got sick. I went rabbit hunting with one of my friends using the rifle that I had brought from the war. Later I gave the rifle to my friend. I kept the Japanese War bayonet and a Japanese flag as souvenirs.

I enrolled at the University of New Mexico to obtain my credits for graduating from High School since I had volunteered for the Army in my Senior Year. I began to look for a job and found one working in a Decorating Studio. I worked there for a few years learning the trade of installing draperies and about the fabric industry which I would use later.

Sleepless Nights at Home

Not long after arriving at home I had been experiencing nightmares all over again. When mom would wake me up, she would find me raised up in bed sweating, and thinking that I was in the jungles of Bougainville again and the enemy after me. It took me a sometime to get over this problem. I continued to go to Mass at the Immaculate Conception Church, where I lost my prayer book Sister Rosita had given me after my first communion at St. Anthony's Orphanage.

College

And though I never officially achieved a "college degree," per se, I am rather certain I completed the level of a degree by the taking of many courses. Ultimately, each related to where the rest of my life's journey would take me. Examples: English at Albuquerque Community College; Logic and Spiritual Direction at the College of Santa Fe; four years part time studies at UNM, including English, Spanish, Counseling, Foundations of Education, and other courses that I thought beneficial to my future growth in Pedagogy, that is, in teaching. I often met my son Stephen on Campus he was attending College also. It was a time of fun. Little did I know that God had great plans for me in the future as a Carmelite Secular member and, as a Deacon of his Church.

In reference to my future service in the Catholic Church from Spiritual Advisor through my final career goal as a Deacon the courses included: Christology, Moral Theology, Church History, Sacraments, Salvation History, Prayer, Psychology, Marriage and Annulment, Canon Law and Homiletics, the art of writing and delivering homilies.

Another aspect of training for the Diaconate would develop into one of my most cherished responsibilities of Church work, even to the current time. And that involved many years of participating in the RCIA program, both as director and instructor. The Rite of Christian Initiation of Adults is a process developed by the Catholic Church many decades ago for prospective converts to Catholicism who are at least seven years of age and are interested in becoming Catholics.

Over the course of several months the Catechumens as they are referred to, are instructed in all aspects of Catholic beliefs and practices. They are presented during the year to the parish congregation at the Sunday masses, as they go through The Rite of Acceptance and The Scrutiny's that prepare them for the Easter Sacraments. In the presence of the Celebrant, they write their names in the Book of the Elect as a pledge of fidelity to Christ. Upon completion of the process, the Elect are conferred upon the parish congregation at the Easter Vigil Mass where they are ceremoniously and joyously welcomed as full members of the Catholic Church, on receiving the sacraments of initiation.

SHE SAID "YES"

Chapter 34

Settling back into civilian life, it was time to start thinking about my future. I was not actively searching for a life partner. I met my future wife on a Sunday afternoon as one of my best friends Sammy as he was called, and I drove down South Broadway Boulevard in Albuquerque. We saw two young women on a Sunday stroll along the sidewalk. I stopped the car and asked if they would like a ride to their destination. Both were very polite, but responded, "no, thank you!"

The identical scenario repeated the following Sunday. Sammy and I were cruising South Broadway again and the selfsame two young girls were strolling down the thoroughfare again. It all seemed like a kind of providential encounter…to me. This time, however, I thought up a new tactic. We asked them if they would like to go for a hamburger and French fries. The one who I had an eye for responded, "you got it!"

I learned in that instant that her name was Consuelo and I guess you might call this chance get-together our first date. Afterwards, we continued to meet up occasionally, just the two of us. However: and from then on, Connie as she liked to be called was never far from my mind.

It did not take long for her to announce that she already had a boyfriend, but that disclosure didn't discourage me a bit. She resided in Gallup, New Mexico, except when she came to Albuquerque to visit and attend Business College. She boarded with a family. After a short time, she returned to her hometown so that I began having to travel there to see her. I motored to Gallup about every two weeks and after a few visits we began to know each other better. My round trip to see her was about 300 miles, but when you are in love, long distances, or any other discomforts, matter not.

After a year of meeting Connie, I proposed and was surprised when she said, "yes!" However, before I could marry her, she said I had to present myself before her uncle and ask for her hand. One of Connie's parents was deceased, and the other still in Mexico, so her uncle was their stand in. I was nervous at first, but he was quite cordial toward me which helped to calm my nerves. we had a long conversation and he finally agreed to approve the marriage.

MARRIAGE AND FAMILY

Chapter 35

Connie, as those closest to her called her, came from a poor family, as did I. She worked at a bank in Gallup, and I was employed by a floor-covering business in Albuquerque. She picked a wedding dress which I bought along with an expensive wedding ring. It was after buying the dress and ring that I sensed that she was beginning to have doubts. A couple of weeks later she announced she was going on a trip to California, I told her if she went there, to forget about the wedding, because this was a few weeks before the wedding. The bridesmaids and other preparations for marriage in the Catholic Church had already been made. She thought it over, changed her mind and did not make the trip after all. I was taking a risk of losing her, but the risk was worth it.

We were married in St. Francis Catholic Church in Gallup with many family members, relatives, and friends on both sides in attendance. We had a big dance, and all had a good time with great food and drinks. We moved into a two-bedroom home I had purchased in Albuquerque with inheritance money from my grandmother. By this time, I had a good job at an interior decorating studio.

Connie and I were faithful to our Catholic commitments, attending Mass on Sundays and Holy Days of Obligation, plus becoming active in parish ministries. Holy Mass was celebrated in an old Army barrack because Our Lady of the Most Holy Rosary Church was a new parish and the main Church had not yet been built. Connie joined the choir as she had a beautiful soprano voice. I became a member of the Holy Name Society and later founded the first parish Conference of the Society of St. Vincent de Paul, a world-wide organization dedicated to serving the poor. In an election of officers, I was elected President of the Holy Name Society, a National Group that honored the Most Holy Name of Jesus. Not many men went to Holy Communion during that time, so one day at Sunday Mass the priest told the men that if they went to Holy Communion as often as Ruben, they would be a good example for the rest of the community. Remember, that on Bougainville during the war I said in prayer to Jesus: "Are you going to let me die here in the jungle without receiving Holy Communion again." I made it a practice to receive Holy Communion often. My hidden life in Christ comes to light not by me but by others. Connie and I often invited poor families to our home to share a meal, and I visited poor families with one of the other members of our Conference. We raised money among our four members by passing a hat to collect funds, but later our pastor, Father Hammer allowed us to serve coffee and donuts on Sunday to raise funds for the poor.

AN UNKNOWN PATH

Chapter 36

Three of our children were born when we lived on 47th Street not far from a Canal. They were Susan, Cathy, and Paul. I left the Decorating Studio after about three years and opened a Window Cleaning Business. I expanded the garage to put my equipment. We hired a baby-sitter as Connie went to work at Sandia Base as a Secretary. she had gone to Business College.

After working about a year, she came home one day upset because one of the employees kept asking her for a date. She said he had been doing this for some time. I told her that I would confront him if she would point him out to me. The following day I went to the Base where she worked and waited as the employees came out of the Security Gate as it was a Government Installation. They came out at 4:30 P.M., and I was a little nervous not knowing who or what kind of man he might be.

As they came out of the gate Connie pointed him out to me. He was not much bigger than me. I confronted him and said: "what do you have against me?" He said: "I have nothing against you" "Then why are you harassing Connie, my wife," I said, and as I spoke, I clenched my fists, and told him, "I am ready to defend my wife now" He replied: "no, no, I will not bother her again." Strangely enough, he was someone I knew from High School. I had to protect my wife as any man would do under the same circumstances. He never bothered Connie again.

We added a large living room and a den to the house. It was then that God began to set me on a different path which included my family by that I mean that not only was I to raise a family but serve Him in service to his Church. I had already begun by helping the poor. "God made me to know him, to love him and to serve him in this world and be happy forever with him in the next."[12]

My mom died at fifty- eight years after a long illness of a heart attack and that was a sad time for us. We buried her at Mount Calvary the same Cemetery that I spoke of when burying others when at St. Anthony's Orphanage. I had given her a Scapular of Our Lady before her death.

One night as I was sleeping in the new den, I had a dream where a beautiful Nun appeared to me. She had a brown Habit (clothing of a Nun). She was behind a grille (forming a barrier or screen) and was trying to hand me something, but as I reached to take it, I woke up. What was she trying to hand me? This was an unusual dream, and it had a message for me.

Two weeks later I was in a doctor's office waiting for my wife as she was in conference with him. I was paging through a Journal, and as I turned the page there was a picture of the same Nun who had appeared to me in my dream two weeks earlier. There was information on who to contact if interested in joining the Religious Order as a lay person or religious. The name on the pictures was that of Saint Therese a Carmelite Nun.

JOINING THE CARMELITE ORDER

Chapter 37

I went to a Catholic Book Store in the downtown area and found three Volumes of what I thought were about St. Therese. I would read at night after coming from work and would read late into the night. It was such wonderful reading that it inspired me to contact Father Howard Rafferty in Chicago Illinois and obtain more information about joining the Carmelite Order the Order of which Saint Therese was a member.

I wrote to Father Rafferty and continued to correspond with him for about a year and asked him if I could be enrolled in the Order. I had shared all this with Connie, and she too began reading the books. He wrote back and said that my wife and I could be enrolled in the Order and be clothed in the large Scapular. The Scapular is six- inches by eight- and, has a large "M" in the front indicating our devotion to Mary and on the back a symbol of the prophet Elijah. The Order of Carmel is dedicated to Mary, The Mother of God. Jesus is her son. He is God. Therefore, Mary is called The Mother of God. Elijah is connected to the Carmelite Order not historically but spiritually. "Elijah ministered to the widow of Zarephath. He restored the life of the widow son who had died, and her jar of oil would not diminish because she had provided him with hospitality.[13]

One Sunday Afternoon

Father Rafferty had the faculties sent to our Paster Father Leo Fay at Holy Rosary Parish together with guidelines for the ceremony of the clothing with the Brown Scapular. On a Beautiful Sunday afternoon with only Father present, Connie and I were clothed in the large Scapular. It is difficult for me to express the joy we experienced. God has many gifts waiting for us in eternity, but He also gives us many here on earth. It was one of the happiest days of my life knowing that we belonged to the Order of Our Lady of Mount Carmel, and the Oder of Saint Therese. The Nuns wear brown and white habits whereas we wear the large Scapular as Secular Order Members. The priests also wear brown Habits. Someone might ask why are you and your wife doing this? Are you not busy raising a family and working to support them? The answer is God comes first in our lives. He tells us in the Gospel that if we put him first everything else will be added on to you. It means a lot to raise our children with a foundation that will help them in this life and prepare them for the next.

TWO ORDERS OF CARMEL

Chapter 38

I discovered later that I had joined an Order of the Carmelites called, the Primitive Order instead of the Discalced Carmelites, and I was unaware that there were two Saint Teresa's in the Order. It was a friend who pointed this out to me that there was a Saint Teresa of Avila and a Saint Therese of Lisieux, and the books that I had been reading were not about Saint Therese of Lisieux they were about Saint Teresa of Avila. Nevertheless, I received many blessing by reading the Works of Saint Teresa of Avila also known as Saint Teresa of Jesus, and I went back to the Book Store and bought a book about Saint Therese of Lisieux titled, "Story of a Soul."

The "Story of a Soul" is not an ordinary book. If you have not read it, you are missing one of the greatest adventures of life, because it is about what God can do with us if we follow his will. Reading this book made me realize that we do not have to do extraordinary feats to win favor with God but to follow the example of Saint Therese her "Little Way of Spiritual Childhood" doing small works with love, faith, humility and confidence in God. We do not fear suffering but join it to "The Passion of Christ."

The devil must have been angry because my wife and I had

joined the Carmelite Order because one night in my dream he appeared and was jumping up and down and vowing that he would get me. He wants a person to look at him even though he is more frightening than the most horrible horror movie you may have ever seen. His mouth is crooked and deformed, and his body is all black from burning in hell. To keep from looking at such a terrible sight, I turned my head to look at a picture of the Immaculate Heart of Mary that I had on a small table next to my bed, and when he saw that I was looking at Mary he disappeared like he did not exist. My wife had been sleeping with the small kids in another room and when she saw me the next morning she said " I sensed that the devil was in our house last night." I said nothing so as not to frighten her.

After about a year I wrote again to Father Howard and told him that I wanted to join the Discalced Carmelites. He wrote and said that the Order I was in had all that I needed to advance in prayer, but after about a year he realized that I was determined to move, and he gave me permission to join the Discalced Carmelites.

A SUNSET MONASTERY

Chapter 39

My reason for transferring is that after reading "The Story of a Soul" and the life of Saint Teresa of Avila I wanted to be in that Order. One day after I came from work, I was reading the newspaper and an article read that the Carmelite Order was about to establish a Convent on Sunset Road which was only about a half mile from our home. There was a Covent in Santa Fe, but this would be in Albuquerque, and I kept thinking how good God is to open a Carmelite Convent so close to where I live. This Covent would be a house of prayer.

Preparations began to be made and I attended the meetings. The meetings were held in the home of the property that had been purchased from a family. It was over an acre and the house had trees that had to be cleared and bushes to be removed. It was a big project and many people offered to help with the renovation of the property. One of my friends who was a carpenter and myself helped with installing doors and other small jobs. One of the large rooms was converted into a chapel with a separate room with a grille where the Nuns could hear Mass. One day as I was exiting the chapel a Carmelite Nun was coming down the entrance path, and as I saw her my heart skipped a beat, and I thought she looks like Saint Therese, but she was the Extern Nun the one who welcomes people. Her name was Sister Margaret Mary. She was liked by all who met her, and when the Covent opened, she would operate the "Turn" from inside a small room that would allow people to place objects on a small circular cabinet that rotated, and to speak with a Nun without being able to see her. Sister Margaret was there to assist in the rooms for the Nuns.

The big day came when the bishop, and other dignitaries arrived for the first Mass to be celebrated in the new Chapel. There was standing room only and the crowd extended to the outer area. It was a great event and the beginning of a House of Prayer.

As my work permitted, I began to assist the priest at Mass, and my family came to worship at the Monastery. We met many new people, and a plan was put in place to provide for the necessary needs of the Nuns. Some of the Nuns that came were from Santa Fe and other parts of the country. The plan for raising funds was called "The Carmel Guild" and proved to be successful and this was due to the members of the community. One of the members was a publisher from back East another two of them were Attorneys and others that had important jobs in the community. We also established a Third Order of Secular Carmelites and, we would meet monthly. One of our leaders was familiar with the Rules of the Third Order as he was already a Carmelite from back East. A Third Order is a group of lay persons who are part of the family of a Religious Order and share in the blessings of the Order. The first order consists of the Priests and Brothers. The second Order are the Nuns, and the third Order are the lay people. For forming a Chapter of lay Carmelites at least thirteen persons is required, and we had that number of persons.

THE CARMEL GUILD

Chapter 40

After the Guild was formed for raising money for the Nuns, I was asked to be the Treasurer, and I accepted. I kept the books as accurately as I could, and we would meet monthly to discuss our receipts and balances, and the proceeds given to the sisters. This meeting was held at a fancy expensive restaurant by the Railway and was known as The Alvarado. I was always very uncomfortable at these meetings because they were professional men, who were wealthy, and I believe they looked down on me as an ordinary worker, although I had my own business. After about two years at Easter Sunday, I brought my family all dressed up with brand new Easter clothes for the Mass at the Monastery. I assisted the priest as the Altar Server, and it gave me great joy with my family and Carmelite members present. Some of the Guild members were also present. Susan, Paul and Cathy were still children and were at Mass with Connie and me. About a day later one of the members called and said they wanted me to hand over the Financial Books of the Guild. I believe they suspected me of stealing funds to buy clothes for my kids for Easter. The upshot is that after checking the books they offered to pay me fifty dollars a month as I had been doing it voluntarily, and I said, I would keep on keeping the books voluntarily. I would take goodies to the Monastery for the sisters once a month, and as I served at Mass, they got to know me without me seeing them, as they were behind the grille. The same kind of grille that I had seen the beautiful Nun in my dream, that I described earlier in the book. Two of the daughters of one of our Third Order members joined the Nuns and began their Postulancy to prepare to make their Vows at the proper time. People from all over the State would come and ask for prayers and brought donations for the Nuns. Their work as Contemplatives attracted other priests to come and say Mass at the Monastery, and I had the privilege of assisting them at Mass.

MOVING NORTH

Chapter 41

Our family was doing well. My business was improving, and I had other employees doing most of the work while I solicited more jobs to keep them busy. Most of the work was getting new homes and new schools ready for occupation.

I had several contracts and would put in a bid for cleaning the structures and often installing drapery hardware. I was happy operating out of my own home, but all began to change when my Sister-in-Law encouraged Connie to move to the Northeast Heights where she and my brother lived, and to buy the latest television set. She would call almost daily, and they took a liking to each other which was fine, but without being judgmental, I looked upon her and my brother as being too worldly. Recall in the early part of my story that my two brothers hated the Orphanage and disliked the sisters. He was a good man, and worked at the Post Office, but as far as I know he was not a practicing Catholic.

I did not want to move, and it would mean that I had to start over again to find a house in the Heights, and it meant moving away from closeness to the Monastery. we had invested our assets in the Valley. My childhood memories of the Northeast Heights were of conflict between Hispanics and Anglo kids. Connie insisted that we move, and it became a family problem and a source of division. She was concerned about the kids, because two of them had breathing problems, but I thought that we could survive the asthma problem, and I was against a television because it might interfere with children's studies. However: in the end she had her way, and we made the move. We found a new house that had just been built, and it had a large garage for my equipment. Connie was happy, and we bought a television. We enrolled the kids in school, but when I came home from work, I would find them watching television.

I continued to attend services at the Carmelite Monastery when I could since now, I was several miles away instead of half a mile. Connie left her job at Sandia Base because of our new baby. We had her baptized and named her Therese after Saint Therese of Lisieux. We had a big celebration and invited many friends.

VATICAN II

Chapter 42

Vatican II was promulgated by Pope Paul VI. It was begun by the Papacy of Saint Pope John XXIII. It has sixteen Documents each one dealing with different important aspects of the Church. It resulted in many changes in the Church. I am concerned only in how it affected the Carmelite Monastery on Sunset Road. I have read the Documents, and they should be studied many times and read commentaries to arrive at the purpose of each one, but because of the changes, in a short time some of the Nuns left the Monastery, and others moved to the Convent in Santa Fe. later I saw two of them working at the Bank.

These were the two daughters of one of our Third Order members who had joined the Monastery, and others also left, and the Monastery was closed. It was a devastating blow to me, and not understanding fully the designs of Vatican II, I blamed myself for failing to go to assist the priests at the Altar and for not visiting the sister as I often did when I lived close by, and it was one of the reasons I did not want to move from the Valley, but my wife insisted even to the point of leaving me. Later I had a better knowledge of Vatican II. Some of the Nuns who served at my Parish also left. One would have to read the Documents to fully understand the full impact that they had on the Church, and how they were interpreted differently by Liturgists, Scholars and Religious leaders. Vatican II had many positive results, and it is still moving the Church forward. In our parish our priest says the Latin Mass on Saturday mornings and some people including me love that Mass. At the Sunset Monastery I would serve Mass and do the servers prayers in Latin. I still study the Vatican II Documents.

A NEW HOME FOR THE THIRD ORDER

Chapter 43

Our Third Order Carmelites closed the Carmel Guild, and we moved our meetings to Saint Charles Borromeo Church on Coal Avenue. It was the home of The Blessed Sacrament Fathers, and they had a Monastery. They were generous to offer us a meeting room, and we continued to meet once a month. They also provided spiritual guidance. The Carmelite life is Christian life, therefore: it is a life of constant conversion as we strive to live in allegiance to and discipleship of Jesus Christ. In this endeavor, the Blessed Virgin Mary is our model and companion. Like her, our call is to a 'hidden union with God' for the sake of the Church and the world. In keeping with our Marian spirit, the primary mission of Carmel is prayer, contemplation, fraternal charity, and apostolic service understood as loving friendship with God. This relationship of intimacy with God, mediated and fostered by Jesus Christ, is the reason or purpose for existence of Carmel.[14]

The family of Carmel has the Priests as the head. They provide spiritual guidance for the Order, conduct retreats, provide training for future Carmelites. The second order are the Nuns. The Secular Order is a part of the Carmelite Family. We have a Father General who resides in Rome. He is head of the Order throughout the world. We have a Provincial and assistants who guide the Secular Order in following the Rule of Carmel.

THE DISCALCED CARMELITES

Chapter 44

Some important elements are at the heart of the Carmelite charism: Contemplative prayer, community, and apostolic service. Fraternal charity is one of the key elements of Carmel. They are embraced in the twelfth century Rule of St. Albert of Jerusalem, which has guided the Order since its inception. Four hundred years later, the Reform Movement, under the leadership of two future Saints and Doctors of the Church. It was to be known as Order of Carmelites Discalced (OCD). It came about by much renown, rapid growth and the upper classes in Spain desiring to have their daughters enroll into such a holy religious order.

In the beginning there was only the "Carmelites of the Ancient Observance." The future Santa Teresa de Ávila was known simply as Doña or Sor Teresa de Ahumada when she took her vows at the Incarnation Convent in Ávila. She later would adopt - as most religious did and still do a name of honor; in her case, Teresa de Jesús which translates to Teresa of Jesus. I am rather certain that during her lifetime "Teresa de Ávila," was not an anticipated name for the future Doctor of the Church.

At the time she entered Carmel, there were more than 150 nuns and postulants in residence at the convent, so that much time had to depend for food and other needs on relatives and visitors coming to the convent. Teresa was disillusioned by the inability to devote time to the contemplative prayer the Rule called for. It was that frustration that energized her to initiate the change of the order.

Along with a handful of other sisters - some quite young - from Incarnation they took the risk. With the help of her well-to-do and respected father, she was able to secure a location in central Ávila for the first of 17 convents she would find throughout Spain, all dedicated to her patron and favorite model, San José (St. Joseph.) She accomplished her Reform of Carmel with the help of Saint John of the Cross. He was interested in the Carthusians, but Teresa told him that he would find all for contemplative prayer in Carmel and, he agreed to participate in the Reform of the Carmelite Order.

The Reform afforded a new direction for the fledgling order, even to the extent of the Convent of the Incarnation eventually joining the Discalced Carmelites. Later Teresa would select Saint, Juan de Yepez y Álvarez- the future San Juan de la Cruz or St. John of the Cross- first as her own spiritual advisor. Presently they both would introduce the reform to the Carmelite Order of Priests.[15]

My devotion to Our Lady of Mount Carmel originated when reading about the Crusaders in the Holy Land. The story of the Little Brothers of Mary and how they struggled to begin a community of contemplatives in a strange country. Some of the Crusaders remained in Israel. after the end of the battle to regain control of the holy places in the holy land. Others were lay people who joined the community.

In the 20th century the Carmelite Order sent professional workers and artists to rebuild the Chapel. After excavations the original site was discovered and, they started to rebuild. The effort took time, and they had to make return trips as their time permitted, only to find out that vandals had destroyed the work that they had done. I kept up with the work being done, but I believe the work was abandoned due to continuous vandalism.

THE SECULAR ORDER OF CARMEL

Chapter 45

The Secular Order of Carmel developed gradually. St. John of Cross's mother Catalina and Francisco his brother, and other lay people followed the priests and nuns of the order by attending Mass and by listening to their teachings. Other religious Orders have lay groups that follow a modified rule according to their state in life. They are called "Oblates" Saint John relates that he had a great love for his brother Francisco. His mother Catalina is one of my favorite Carmelites. In time the Secular Order was originally known as Third Order Members and later the name became Secular Carmelites. Our Acronym is OCDS.

After many months of taking classes together with my brothers and sisters of Carmel at the chapel of the Monastery on Sunset Road, and after having made my vows with some of the other members, eventually I made my Definitive Promise, after three years as a Secular Carmelite in 1956. The Definitive Promise means that a person has developed in his/her quest as a Carmelite for life and to follow its rules according to their state in life as married, single or widowed.

In addition, after much studying and by a recommendation by Dr. Joyce Rogers, who was President of our Chapter of Holy Cross asked me to be a Presenter at a workshop on John of the Cross's Family, at San Diego State University in California during a Carmelite Retreat. I also attended other Carmelite convocations at St. Joseph's Monastery in San Jose, California, a Leadership Conference in Seattle, and a Spiritual Directors' seminar at the University of New Mexico Newman Center under the direction of a priest on spiritual matters. My experience with Contemplative Prayer is that it is a gradual work. There are times when one needs a priest with experience in the deeper spiritual life to ((protect the postulant). A Postulant is one who aspires to join the Order for membership. Protection is needed against the wiles of the devil. In this kind of prayer an aspirant becomes more aware of the love of God, and the need for direction in the spiritual life. It is true that the writings and teachings of St. John of the Cross and St. Teresa of Jesús (Ávila) cover most aspects of the Spiritual Life, but they also warn of "poor directors who can lead a person astray"[15]. In my case, it seemed the more I continued to read and meditate on the works of John of the Cross "The Ascent of Mount Carmel" and "The Spiritual Canticle" - along with "The Foundations" of Saint Teresa, including "The Interior Castle", I began to experience attacks by the devil attempting to prevent me from following the way of Carmel. After consultation with one of the Blessed Sacrament Priests who was a contemplative, I began to have more confidence in my prayer life.

ST. THERESE OF LISIEUX

Chapter 46

St. Therese played a great part in my story as a Secular Carmelite as well as The Blessed Virgin Mary of Mount Carmel. After reading her book "The Story of a Soul" made me realize that we are made for a life of heaven. We are to struggle against the temptations within our own selves and the world the flesh and the devil. But her story changed my life, that I may have confidence and trust in God.

Her "Little Way," her way of doing little things for God, and for missionaries, for example, she wants to be "a small toy for God," and He can do with her according to His will.[16]. Her Oblation of prayer of her sacrifice of her life for God is a powerful example of her love for Him.

I could not share some of my experiences with my wife while she had her hands full with our children. She would attend the Carmelite meetings with me and enjoyed the company of other women, but she had no idea that I was being troubled by the evil one. Only on one occasion, upon waking in the morning, did she share that she had sensed the "devil in the house" during the night. I was certain that Satan was trying to cause a division between us. And it was not easy for her; we had lost one child who lived only three days and who we named Louis Martin after the father of St. Thérèse of Lisieux, the Little Flower. One night the day of the death of Louis our baby the devil appeared to me in my sleep in an ugly form, so ugly that it troubled me the only thing that kept his face away from me was my scapular and remembering the face of baby Louis Martin.

When the devil appears, he wants us to look at him. We must not bother looking his mouth is twisted and has a face like a vicious growling dog. In retrospect, I realized that my problem might have been psychological or something that could readily be solved by a psychiatrist. But when a person is deeply serious about following Jesus, he/ she may or will encounter attacks by the devil. Jesus told Peter that the evil one had tried to destroy him (Peter), but that He had prayed for him[17].

In his First Letter, Peter says: "Be sober and vigilant, your opponent, the devil, is prowling around like a roaring lion looking for someone to devour; resist him, be steadfast in faith…"[18]

It is by our Baptism and by living a life of faith that we can conquer the evil one. As one priest told us, "Tell the devil to go away." Another priest said: "tell him to go to hell" (Father John Fitzgerald, Assistant Pastor at Queen of heaven Parish) Saint Teresa of Ávila does say that we must spend more time with Jesus then bothering with the devil…I continued studying the works of John and Teresa, plus other treatises and tracts on spirituality and many others penned by Carmelite authors. I attended workshops from California to Arkansas; was on hand at retreats, listening to many lectures and reading every Carmelite composition I could get my hands on. Yet, even with all that, I still felt, and even today continue to sense, that I am still on the journey. There is no doubt that the Works of the Saints of Carmel are a great help and give direction to our contemplative journey because they went through it and give examples of the way we must follow.

SILENT PRAYER AND LECTIO DIVINA

Chapter 47

Silent Prayer is required by the Ruled of Carmel. It was given to us by Saint Albert Patriarch of Jerusalem. The Rule defines the way, the goal, which separate the Rule of one Order from another. He gave us this Rule in the Thirteenth Century. Silent prayer may be preceded by spiritual reading from the Bible, the Psalms, or some book on spiritual themes. I still prepare ahead of time for silent prayer because, I am not at the stage of a proficient that John of the Cross speaks about. We are to spend half hour a day in silent prayer, and I relaxed my duty for several years as a result I am behind in the stage where I should be at.

Silent prayer leads to union with God by faith, and brings with it much peace, but before union a person may undergo many trials and even suffering before arriving at this union. A person needs direction by a learned priest when embarking on such a lofty way. There are many books on this subject one of the best being the Works of Saint Teresa of Ávila, John of the Cross, Thomas Merton, and other spiritual authors who can guide one through the various stages of contemplative prayer. As I say, I am still practicing silent prayer and I make time for my meeting with God in faith and love. Contemplative prayer leads to growth in faith and love of God and neighbor. If more people would practice prayer, they would find more meaning in their lives and, prepare for their meeting with God in eternity. It removes much of the fear of death because a person is already conversing with God in silence. If you really need an example of silence look to Saint Joseph. Not everyone who practices contemplative prayer will have union with God in this life only God knows why.

Prayer before the Blessed Sacrament is highly recommended by bishops and priests for the faithful as a way of closeness to God and for gaining many graces. First Friday devotions take place in many parishes.

Mary-lake Monastery

My community of Carmel sent me to Arkansas to Mary-lake I was sent for a workshop on Lectio Divina which means "divine reading." There were four priests, two postulants, studying for the priesthood, and several Secular Carmelites present for the conference.

The Church where the meeting was held is huge and constructed of stone; a beautiful Cathedral-medieval like structure, with several floors. I remember a stunning painting of St. Thérèse of the Child Jesus on the stairway leading to the second floor. She almost seemed alive it was so grand. I was at the conference for a week, attending Mass daily and studying with the group and learning about the sacred tradition of Lectio Divina prayer.

Lectio Divina has four important elements: reading, meditation, prayer and contemplation. Father Sam Anthony Morello points out that there is not distinctively Teresian way to pray…Carmel's spirituality is rooted in the greater tradition of Lectio Divina (literally, "divine reading"), a particular way of reading and praying over the Scriptures.

"The word of God moves from the lips to the mind, and now into the heart."[19]

One night something very mystical happened. I arose not being able to sleep and decided to take a walk in the darkness and suddenly found myself about to fall down some stairs. Only by the grace of God was I able to grab onto something that stopped me from descending into the dark stairwell. In the morning I went back to check the area and found where I had almost fallen. I discovered that if I had fallen it would have been doubtful that anyone could have found me, for the stairs led to a dark, deep cellar. I thanked my Guardian Angel for protecting me. This experience reminded me of the time I was in a storm on the Destroyer off Cebu in the Philippines and how my Guardian Angel helped me grab a railing that prevented me from going into the ocean. When I returned from the conference, I reported to my community all I had learned about Lectio Divina.

Summarizing my Contemplative Prayer experience, I would say that not getting fully into it and struggling so much was my fault entirely because of my lack of private, silent prayer. The Rule in Carmel is that we are to spend a half hour of silent prayer each day. In addition, I let the devil plague me for a long time due to his knowing my weaknesses and continually deceiving me with pleasures of the world and of the past. Thank God I was able to overcome useless temptations. St. John of the Cross says: "only God can deliver us from such dangers.[20]

I continue with my silent prayer and with the help of Our Blessed Mother, just as she had done in the jungles of Bougainville, Leyte, and Cebu, I persevere in my life as a Carmelite, following its Rule. I still present the "Lectio Divina" prayer to other groups.

DEVOTION TO ST JOSEPH AND RELICS OF ST THERESE

Chapter 48

Devotion to Saint Joseph began for me when I was at Saint Anthony's Orphanage. The Nuns would pass out holy pictures of the saints and one of them was Saint Joseph. Devotion to the saint grew when Saint Teresa of Ávila named all her Monasteries in his name. She lavished great honor on him and said that he always answered her prayers. There are many stories of how this saint has helped those in trouble or when in great need, for example, when I was working late in my office one night he appeared to me, and without saying anything he made known to me to go home. In other words, my family needed me, and I obeyed and did as he ordered me. The Order of Carmel honors Saint Joseph by naming Churches and other places of prayer in his name. In my Parish at Queen of Heaven the Pastor asked the staff what should, we name the new building that had been constructed for evening classes. No one said anything, so I suggested "name it Saint Joseph's Building" that is the name of the building to this day.

The story of Saint Joseph in the Bible is very powerful in that he protected Jesus and Mary when King Herod had plans to kill him. He took them to Egypt where the Jews had been slaves of the Pharoah for four hundred years, and they remained there for about three years, and then returned to Nazareth. Joseph also taught Jesus the carpenter's trade, and Jesus was happy to be known as the "Son of the Carpenter." We do not know when Joseph died, but his silence speaks volumes. He teaches us that silence is often the best answer.

<u>A Letter to the Carmel at Lisieux</u>

As my Carmelite devotion developed, I felt the need for further growth and support from my new community. I wrote to the Carmel convent, the cloister at Lisieux in France, where I knew that Thérèse and three of her four sisters, all Carmelite nuns, had resided. I addressed the letter to sister Genevieve of the Most Holy Face, who was the next older sister of Thérèse, four years her senior and closest confidante. Her given name was Marie Celine but had taken Genevieve as her religious order appellation. I explained in my letter that I was a Third Order Carmelite, included a donation and asked for prayers for me and my family. This was in the late 1950's.

The Nuns wrote back saying that Sister Genevieve was quite ill, but that she would offer prayers for us. In fact, she died in 1959. As a quite generous gesture, they sent two relics, one that had touched the body of Thérèse, who had died in 1897 at the age of 24 and a second one of Santa Teresa de Jesús, (Ávila). A relic is an object that belonged to a saint be it a bone or cloth that touched the body of the saint. These relics are called sacramentals and are very powerful in asking for prayer from the saints and, warding off evil spirits. There are first class relics, second class, and third class. I still have the relic of the Saint Therese but lost the one of St. Teresa when my family moved to another house. Today I persist in being grateful for the kindnesses shown to me by the Carmelite nuns of Lisieux. I continue sharing my relic with Secular Carmelites at our meetings and other religious events. Mine are second class relics.

Several years ago, major relics of Saint Thérèse were brought from France for a United States tour. Albuquerque was included among many towns, cities, and states. One of our local Carmelites went to Kansas to retrieve them for veneration here. They were displayed with much devotion from New Mexican Catholics, at Immaculate Conception Church in downtown Albuquerque. Our Carmelite Secular Order was put in charge of guarding them as people from all over came to honor the Little Flower, St. Thérèse of the Child Jesus.

It was in reading her autobiography, The Story of a Soul, that I began to have great devotion to Saint Thérèse and deep reverence for her parents Louis and Zelie Martin. Likewise, (admiration for three of her siblings, all Lisieux Carmelite nuns.

Marie Louise (22 February 1860 – 19 January 1940), known as Sister Marie of the Sacred Heart[21]
Marie Pauline (7 September 1861 – 28 July 1951), Mother Agnès of Jesus[22]
Marie Leonie (3 June 1863 – 16 June 1941), Sister Françoise-Thérèse, Visitation School at Caen; candidate for sainthood since January 2015; (Francoise-Therese) is the only sister of The Little Flower who did not become a Discalced Carmelite, instead took the religious habit at the Monastery of the Visitation. In honor and memory of her sister St. Thérèse, took her sibling's birth name Marie François-Thérèse[23]

Marie Céline (28 April 1869 – 25 February 1959), now known as Sister Geneviève of the Most Holy Face, closest sister and confidante to Thérèse.[24]

And finally the Saint herself, Marie Françoise-Thérèse (2 January 1873 – 30 September 1897), chosen religious name: Thérèse of the Child Jesus and of the Holy Face, (aka: The Little Flower) and Thérèse of Lisieux, canonized in 1925, [25]

The Infant Jesus of Prague

In Carmel we have devotion to the Infant Jesus of Prague. In Carmelite convents you will find a statue of the Infant beautifully dressed in Kingly attire. Legend has it that; the statue was created by a Monk who based it on an apparition. It is said that Saint Teresa owned it at one point. There is a long history behind the statue, but many convents make their own. The Carmelites in Santa Fe, New Mexico have a statue of the Infant. By honoring the infant, we honor the mystery of the Incarnation and the infancy of Jesus. The Infant Jesus of Prague is the Patron Saint of children, colleges, family, Foreign Missions, and vocations The original is in Prague of the Czech Republic. The devotion was approved by Pope Pius X. Pope Benedict XVI during his visit to the Czech Republic granted a Canonical Coronation to the image in September 2000.[26]

There are several novenas to the Infant Jesus of Prague.

MENTAL ILLNESS

Chapter 49

I must now come to a chapter in my life that is difficult to write about, but I must tell the truth because as I understand it the core of society is the family, and I believe the evil one was creating a division within our family. I have no other way of explaining why with all the benefits that God was granting us, and my devotion to the Church that things would take the wrong turn.

I must bear much of the responsibility because I was also interested in sports. As I said before from the beginning, I did not want a television in my home, but to keep peace in the family I agreed to it. I was divided spending time in prayer, but also watching sports on TV, and became interested in football, basketball, and tennis. I looked upon it as a way of relaxing, but playing tennis became an obsession, and I learned how to play the game well, and began to play in tournaments at the tennis courts. I would arrange my work schedule so that I could spend much time at the tennis court and even got my son Stephen playing the game so that later he was in the High School Tennis Team.

I did not attend the Carmelite meetings as often and slacked off on the half hour of silent prayer that was part of the rule of Carmel. It is no wonder that things began to change. The choices I made were not good. In a dream I was playing tennis, and suddenly, I fell on the concrete and died. my friends carried me off in a white sheet. I woke up and unable to get back to sleep and knew that God was not happy with me. I had to make sone changes.

My wife had been helping me with the business. She was a do it all, secretary, sales lady, bookkeeper. We had four women making the draperies. I had moved my business from the home to a store on one of the main streets. I still had employees for the window cleaning business and one helper for the drapery installations. Connie loved the work because she had company with the women employees, and she and I took turns at picking up the kids from school and taking them to music lessons, etc.

After about three years we moved the store to Eubank Northeast, and we were doing well until she got sick. She lost interest in the business and gradually lost interest for the family. The family thought that things would work out, but they did not. She got worse and at times would get violent and could not be controlled. She would not speak to me, and I became concerned about the safety of the children and myself, it got that bad. I believe that she was mad at God because she broke our beautiful statue of Our Lady of Mount Carmel. We decided to put her in a Mental Hospital, and she agreed. She would come home from time to- time but only to return to the Hospital. She made friends at the hospital but would not talk to me. What turned her against me I could not figure out, but I thought the devil was dividing our family that was centered in Christ. Connie was a good wife and mother and cared about her children.

She was an important part of the business, and due to her sickness and her leaving, my business endeavors began to fall apart. It was a question of cash flow. Most of our income went for payroll. Paying the rent for the business was also a priority. I got behind in the home mortgage and other bills. My main concern was to pay the women, and the men who worked for us, and to pay the taxes. I took care of all that, but when I tried to pay the home mortgage they demanded three payments, and I did not have the money. With all the pressure and stress on both of us I decided to declare Bankruptcy. I did sell some of the assets to pay some bills, and to have some cash for emergencies.

When we lost the house Connie decided to go to Gallup, by herself. I gave her enough money for the trip and food. I tried to convince her to come with me, and the three small children to California, but she refused. Our older children were on their own and doing well. I made arrangement with my cousin in California to put us up until I could get a job, and he agreed. I could have done things differently, but I had mixed emotions at the time and wanted to help Connie as much as I could.

ON THE ROAD

Chapter 50

The children and I packed up and headed for California a day after Connie had gone to Gallup where her sister lived with her family. We went to her sister's home who lived in the South part of the town, but was told that she had rented a motel, so I went to the motel and pleaded with her to come with us, but again she refused. I do not know if it was her illness that kept her from coming with us or was confused. All this time she would not talk to me, my kids were my interpreters.

The kids and I stayed with my cousin in Long Beach, California. He had a two-story Home, and we occupied the second floor. I got a job at a Furniture Store in Los Angeles. There was a Catholic Church next door, and the Blessed Sacrament was exposed. During my lunch hour I would visit Our Lord, and prayed that our situation with the family would be resolved.

After a few weeks I called Connie's uncle in Orange County, and asked him if he could help me bring Connie to California. He hesitated, but after thinking about it he decided to help. I had helped him when he had a car accident in Gallup many years earlier and, recommended an Attorney who was a Carmelite Third Order member and who got him a good settlement.

We went on a Weekend to Gallup and found Connie in the Motel. He had to talk to her for some time and convinced her that she was not safe living alone, and that she must return to her family. She came back to California with us, and I moved the family to

Watts a suburb of Los Angeles where Connie had relatives. It was in the winter and there was no heat in the house. I kept my job at the store, and we enrolled the kids in school. And on my time off I joined the Saint Vincent De Paul Conference to help other poor families. I also began teaching Catechism to the school children after school. They allowed it as it was out in the playground. Connie kept busy with her cousins who lived across the street.

About two months later I found an apartment in Los Angeles' It was closer to my job, and the family was happier. Later, the Company where I worked decided to transfer me to West Covina about forty miles away to take charge of a drapery department, since I had experience in that field. The pay was fair, and I managed to save some money as the rent was reasonable. After working there about a year, I came home one night, and the kids said that their mom was gone. We went out looking for her, and a Policeman helped us look for her, and we found her roaming around confused. She had gone out for ice cream and, had been assaulted by a stranger who did some injuries to her. We took her to a hospital, and she was there several days. Due to her mental illness, she did not seem concerned about what had happened. When we visited her at the hospital she appeared with a male friend and still would not talk to me.

I heard from the Attorney about the Bankruptcy by phone, and he said that I must return home, if I wanted to finish the paperwork on the Bankruptcy otherwise, he would drop the case. I would have to find another Attorney. I made plans to send Connie and my son Stephen back to Albuquerque. We both knew a family that agreed to help us until my return, and I would reimburse them for any expenses. I sent them by train hoping that all would be well.

After working about six more months, I packed up and began the journey back home with Therese and Dominic my two children. It was driving up the San Bernardino Mountains that became a serious problem due to the van that I had driven many miles commuting to West Covina and now was sputtering as we drove up the steep mountain. The van appeared like it was about to stop running. I prayed and asked the kids to pray, and as we neared the top it made a last gasp and we barely made it, after that it was down all the way. Our prayers were answered.

MOVING FORWARD

Chapter 51

We arrived in town, and I picked up Connie and Stephen and thanked the couple who helped us and promised to pay them back. We settled in the Northeast section. I rented a three-bed- room house that was not furnished. I bought a bed for Connie and Therese, but Dominic, Stephen and I had to sleep on the concrete floor. That night as Dominic, Stephen and I were sleeping had a dream where a beautiful man with a white beard appeared and again as before he looked like the painting of God by Michelangelo that is in the Vatican. He stretched his arms to receive me. I stretched my arms upward to grab his arms, but suddenly my arms fell, and I woke up. I did not know what to make of the dream, but it was a consolation from God assuring me that all was going to be well. The following day I found a job at a Decorating Store. Connie was still uncertain about her life with me. I wondered that if I had shared my experiences of the devil constantly attacking me, she would have had a better understanding of what I had experienced and might have helped her in her illness by being more patient.

The upshot of this is that within a few months I saw a house for sale and contacted the realtor. I explained to her about the Bankruptcy, but she said if I was a Veteran that she could help me. She was a kind and smart about the Real Estate Law because she was able to help me buy the house with the help of my boss at J.C. Penney who wrote a letter to the Mortgage Company indicating that I had a future with the Company. This made a big difference in my wife's disposition. She began to be happy again and, loved the house with the two big trees in the back yard. She began to make plans to decorate the home. Now I was able to continue my payer life for the good of the family.

CARMEL AND THE DIACONATE

Chapter 52

It was through one of our Carmelite members that I began to assist the priests at the Diagnostic Center for Juveniles on Saturday evenings when they said Mass for Catholic youths. Margaret was the name of the Carmelite who told me that they needed someone to assist the priest with Mass and Catechism instruction. I faithfully assisted for eleven years when Father Landry, a Jesuit, encouraged me to study for the Diaconate. I did not know anything about the Diaconate, but a year later he reminded me again and, he wrote me a letter of recommendation which I took to my Pastor at Queen of Heaven Parish. The Pastor said he would recommend me if I made it a priority. I agreed. I was attending UNM part- time in the evenings and working full time. The Pastor's approval is required as well as being active in ministry.

SPIRITUAL WARFARE CONTEMPLATIVE PRAYER

Chapter 53

What is Spirituality?

Spirituality according to Websters Ninth Collegiate Dictionary is "sensitivity or attachment to religious values." "The quality or state of being spiritual," and according to Robert P. Maloney, CM, "spirituality is an energizing vision, a driving force. It is on the other hand, the specific way in which he or she relates to the created world. It is an insight as the source of action. For the Christian, it is a way of seeing Christ and being in him that directs the individual's energies in the service of the kingdom."[27]

I had been reading the writings of Saint John of the Cross for an extended period and at times found myself fearful of sleeping at night because he often speaks of the devil's attacks on those who try to seek union with God. One priest said to us at a meeting: "If you are a Carmelite you are going to be tempted." Father Phillison wrote fifty pages on the dangers of the present-day concerning signs of the devil in our secular society.

In maintaining that practice, I want to relate an incident that occurred. In Chapter 16 of the Spiritual Canticle, one of St. John's major pieces, I learned how the devil tries by many horrors and torments to intimidate a person who prays. I was not at that time experienced of deep spiritual issues.

At that time, my job took me to a home in the Northeast Heights of Albuquerque to deliver and install draperies. At the time I was sub-contracting this work with another firm. I knocked on the door and a lady responded. She startled me with the question, "you are not afraid of lizards, are you?" I answered "no!"

As I walked into the living room a hellish beastlike creature was coming toward me. It was about four feet tall and resembled a devil...or so I thought. I had never in my life seen such a horrible and grotesque monstrosity. I was very frightened and told the lady that I could not do the installation unless she took the demon away. She stated, "It's my pet and I will put it in my bedroom." However, as I continued with the installation, I felt compelled to keep an eye out for the possible return of the critter. I suppose reading about the horrors of the devil the night before had a lot to do with my reaction to the lizard, but I felt a connection between the two experiences. I later learned that the feral pet was an Iguana, a type of lizard found in Mexico and the Caribbean. Had I known that earlier, I might have not been so disturbed.

Another inspiring aspect of Carmel is that when inducted into the Secular Order, one must choose a special Carmelite name. I chose "Louis Martin" after St. Therese's father; Consuelo chose "Anna María of the Little Flower of Jesus," thus the explanation of those names being on a letter we received in January of 1957 from Mother Helen Marie and her sisters from the Monastery.

Many Years Ago

Many years ago, I had a dream that was real in its lesson. By that I mean that there are things in my life that had to be changed for me to advance not only in my daily work but in my spiritual endeavor. In the dream I saw many faces of people mounted on what appeared to be posts buried in the ground and rising about six feet above the ground. Their faces were moving from side to side in unison, but they could not speak or hear. They seemed able to see but were unable to move except wagging their heads from side to side. It was a sad spectacle and there was nothing that could be done for them because they made choices in life such as worshipping idols. It reminded me of something that one would see in a carnival, but the faces were of real-life persons. I learned from this dream to keep away from false idols. I have written a poem about this dream based on Psalm 135: v. 15-18.[28]

> *"The idols of the nations are.*
>
> *Silver and gold,*
>
> *the work of human hands.*
>
> *They have mouths but do not.*
>
> *speak:*
>
> *they have eyes but do not see:*
>
> *They have ears but do not hear:*
>
> *nor is their breath in,*
>
> *their mouths,*
>
> *Their makers will become like*
>
> *them,*
>
> *and anyone who trusts in them,,,"*

As I continued attempting to comprehend the theology of St. John of the Cross, I had some unusual dreams which seemed more supernatural than anything else. For example: In one dream the devil appeared with all his ghastly ugliness and jumping up and down intimating that he would get me. I had a picture of the Immaculate Heart of Mary on my nightstand. Upon looking at it intently, the devil suddenly was gone. Another time, I dreamt he came outside our parish hall at Queen of Heaven Church. He searched all overlooking up for me, but I was below where he could not see me. When I awoke, I realized that if we are sincerely humble of heart, he cannot find us. In chapter sixteen of his Spiritual Canticle, John of the Cross states that the devil will try all kinds of horrors to keep the bride from having union with the bridegroom, who is Christ.[29]

The Wild Great Danes

On a contract job I went to an expensive home to do drapery work, and I was told no one would be home, but to lock the house after I finished. I drove up unloaded my tools and, put some of the materials in the back yard. I proceeded with the work in the living room and went out to the back yard to get some of the drapery rods. Suddenly out nowhere two vicious Danes came after me growling and barking. I grabbed the rods and ran for the door and barely made it inside, but their huge mouths were inside the door trying to bite me. I kept trying to force them out, but they were vicious and fierce and could almost grab my hands as I tried to push them out. The struggle went on for about eight minutes and they gave up and I closed the door.

Later I told the designer about the incident, and he said, "you were very lucky because they would have killed you." Again, I thanked God for his marvelous protection ("keep me safe; O God, in you I take refuge" (Psalm 16)).

Not long after that the devil threatened me again this time, he showed me that I was in hell, and he was using a weapon to strike again and again, as I was lying on a hot bed of steel. Of all the attacks on me this was the most frightening of all because there was fire all around, and he made it seem like there was no escape from that place, and I was there forever, but I woke up suddenly I believe my Guardian Angel, or Our Blessed Mother woke me. I turned to prayer immediately. I was so distressed. What is the lesson for me.? I believe that I must continue my prayers, especially silent prayer. "The malicious demons on their part disturb the soul in two ways: they vehemently incite and stimulate these appetites and by means of them and other imaginations, etc., wage war on this peaceful and flowering kingdom of the soul." "In the second way, which is worse, they assail her with bodily torments and noises to distract her, when it is impossible for them to do so in the first way. And what is still worse they struggle against her with spiritual terrors and horrors that sometimes become a frightful torment."[30]

Man with a Rifle

On another incident I was sent to do a job in a rural area where there were a few trailer homes. I got out of my van and proceed to enter the gate of the home but, saw a man pointing a rifle at me daring me to enter. I knew from my military experience that you do not challenge someone who is armed and could be dangerous.

He kept staring at me, and I decided to call the office of the company that sent me out. the woman who answered told me to get out of there as fast as I could. I did that and wondered if she knew something I did not know. Perhaps his house had been broken into or he was defending his territory.

ST. TERESA'S VISION

Chapter 54

Saint Teresa of Ávila had visions of the evil one attaching her. She says that God showed her a place in a dark dungeon-like tunnel. She was right above a slimy river with all kinds of ugly creatures, and she could not move, or she would fall into the slimy place full of snakes, toads, scorpions and other ugly creatures. I quote what she said:

"I was at prayer one day, when suddenly without knowing how, I found myself, I thought, plunged right into hell. I realized that it was the Lord's will that I should see the place which the devils had prepared for me there and which I had merited for my sins. This happened in the briefest space of time…the entrance, I thought, resembled a very long, narrow passage, like a furnace, very low, dark, and closely confined, the ground seemed to be full of water which looked like filthy, evil-smelling mud, and in it were many wicked-looking reptiles. At the end there was a hollow place scooped out of a wall, like a cupboard, and it was here that I found myself in close confinement. But sight of all this was pleasant by comparison with what I felt there. … I felt a fire within my soul the nature of which I am utterly incapable of describing. My bodily sufferings were so intolerable that, though in my life I have endured the severest sufferings of this kind-the worst it is possible to endure, the doctors say, such as the shrinking of the nerves during my paralysis…the agony of my soul, an oppression, a suffocation and an affliction so deeply felt, and accompanied by such hopeless and distressing misery…

to say that it is as if the soul were continually being torn from the body is very little, for that would mean that one's life was being taken by another, whereas in this case it is the soul itself that is tearing itself to pieces.

The fact is I cannot find words to describe that interior fire, and that despair, which is greater than the most grievous torment and pains. I could not see who the cause was, but I felt, I think, as if I were being both burned and dismembered: and I repeat that that interior fire and despair are the worst thing of all.

In that pestilential spot, where I was quite powerless to hope for comfort, it was impossible to sit or lie, for there was no room to do so. I had been put in a place which looked like a hole in the wall, and those very walls, so terrible to the sight bore down upon me and completely stifled me. There was no light, and everything was in the blackest darkness. I did not understand how this can be, but although there was no light, it was possible to see everything the sight of which can cause affliction. At that time, it was not the Lord's will that I should see more of hell, but I have since seen another vision of frightful things"[31]

APPLYING FOR THE DIACONATE

Chapter 55

Following the advice of my Pastor and Father Landry I attended the first meeting for Deacon candidates of the Archdiocese of Santa Fe, New Mexico. There were many men interested in the Diaconate. We were told that we would be interviewed and, we would be notified if accepted or not. It would be determined by the result of the interview.

The first Deacon and his wife who came to my home to interview me gave me a "thumbs up" review, although the questions they asked were many about our marriage, our children, my work, my prayer life and my education.

The second Deacon and his assistant were, I believe, ready to approve me after about two hours of questioning, but my wife did not agree. She told the couple who interviewed us that "she loved me just as I was. She said, "I do not want him up there preaching." I took her first comment as a compliment, but her second comment surprised me, and I was not chosen for the classes. If the wife does not approve the person will not be allowed to attend classes and would not be ordained. My wife was not in her best health at the time.

My drapery and Window Cleaning projects were doing well. I hired a man who had only one arm for washing windows. He would brush the window with water, and then use the squeegee to finish, all with one arm. I also hired a man who was handicapped. He had one leg shorter than the other. I hired a High School student who also was a good worker. These men had families and needed work. I had contracts with some Government Agencies who were encouraged by their policies to deal with small businesses, and I got contracts to clean the outside windows of several four- story buildings. The work was risky, and I hired others for the job. I had to get security clearance for them, for it was in a sensitive area of the Government's Projects and, I provided insurance papers for everyone's protection. I also did some drapery work for one of their theatres with automatic switches for smooth operation.

THE DARK MOUNTAIN

Chapter 56

In the center of all this work something else was at work within me. One night in a dream I saw a huge mountain covered with smoke coming towards me with great force and, the face of a strong bearded man in the cloud. It was frightening. The face of the man was like a picture of the face of God I had seen in a journal perhaps a copy of Michelangelo's painting that is in the Vatican. I woke up from the dream and could not go back to sleep. I kept thinking, what does this dream mean?

In the morning I was about to enter the bathroom, but my nineteen- year son Dominic was already there getting ready for work, and the door was open. He was combing his hair and looking at himself in the mirror when he saw me. We looked at each other just for an instant, but there was something mysterious about the look that we exchanged. He seemed that he wanted to tell me something, but he said nothing. Did this exchange of looks have something to do with the dark mountain in my dream and, face of a man that resembled God?

Yes, it did. Six hours later Dominic was dead. God had warned me ahead of time in his great mercy and goodness that something life changing was about to happen.

This is how it happened. Our son was working for a furniture store, and he and his boss and another employee had gone to unload furniture from a Railway boxcar located about a mile from our home. The door of the boxcar was stuck, and they could not open it, so the boss tied a chain from the door of the boxcar to his truck and drove the truck to open the door, but it did not open it fell off its hinges and fell on top of Dominic. He was injured severely. I was at work when the police called me at about two-o-'clock in the afternoon, and the officer said: "there has been an accident your son is in the hospital, go as soon as you can." I got in my car and headed for the hospital which was a few miles from where I was. I was unaware of the horrible accident. I kept thinking I hope he did not wreck the car.

I believe that was my way of calming myself down. I did not this time, associate any happening with my dream the previous night. As I arrived at the hospital members of my family met me looking shocked and apprehensive but said nothing. I knew then that something was very wrong.

We waited a long time for the doctor to share information, and when he came, he said, "We tried to save him and, other doctors trying to help him, but we could not do it. His heart had burst from the weight of the train door. He said the door weighed about a thousand pounds.

There is no way to describe the pain in the face of my wife and children. I kept thinking of the dream of the huge mountain on smoke and a human face in the cloud. I never told my family about the dream because I felt the accident happened on account of my sins and my lack of participation in my Carmelite vocation.

The funeral for Dominic was held at Queen of Heaven Parish with a priest that had recently arrived at our Parish. He was very kind and said that in God's eyes it was a full life for Dominic. During the Mass my pain was unbearable, and I kept looking at the cross on the wall behind the Altar. One of our friends kept repeating "have faith." Many people came to offer their condolences as well as students from Del Norte High School where Dominic graduated. He was a student of guitar and was proficient, and I thought he had a great future ahead of him. The student choir sang a song I had never heard before it was called "Time in a Bottle" or something like it. I think it was written by Jim Croce. I thought that I could have done something to prevent his death, and the song stayed in my mind for many days. A bottle may be used for many things, but not for putting time in it however: the song may me think about the death of our son.

DEATH OF CONNIE

Chapter 57

I cannot say enough about my wife. Consuelo was a very vivacious person and had an engaging personality. From the very beginning of our life together she was a hard-working soul mate. She loved and nurtured the children and did all she could to foster their education. They were well-behaved, although like most kids of their day, at times sought recreation in the way most kids of their age did, but after our son's death her health turned bad. I took her to the doctor since she had not been feeling well, and the doctor surprised us by saying that she had cancer of the Uterus. He would have to start Cancer treatments immediately. She almost fainted and started to cry. I was distressed and quietly prayed for courage. I said to her that we would get through this trial. I made plans to pay for her treatments as we did not have insurance, I tried to put her on an insurance plan years earlier and she refused, but I did have some stock with the Electric Company to pay the doctor, so that the treatments began right away. Our family took it hard, but our faith in God carried us through the months of dealing with the dreaded disease. While she was being treated at the hospital by radiation the family could go and see her one at a time and were to stay far from her. One day I was there alone, and she looked so sad looking at me that I went straight to her and held her hand. As she got worse, they sent her home, and the family began taking turns caring for her. The end came sooner than expected. She received the Last Sacraments of the Church by Father John

Fitzgerald a good friend of the family. She lived for seven years after the dearth of Dominic. Her funeral was held at Queen of Heaven Parish and was buried at Mount Calvary next to our son Dominic. My wife had many friends. And the Church was packed for her funeral.

Family Portrait

Susan, our eldest, graduated from Del Norte High School in Albuquerque. Later in life she became a writer of religious themes and distributed them all over the world. She married and had five children.

Therese took piano lessons and loved to run; she is a graduate of UNM in Business Administration and worked at Sandia Labs, and at a Designing Studio.

Cathy was more reserved but friendly and did well in school; she worked in a bakery and a manufacturing plant. As she got older, she took her religion seriously and even joined a group ministering to incarcerated individuals. Her group visited the Prison in Los Lunas.

Paul was scientific-minded and became an engineer. He worked for PNM and other firms in Arizona. He married and had three children.

Dominic graduated from High School and Liked to play the guitar. He had many friends and enjoyed playing with a group. He died at nineteen years in an accident.

Stephen is the youngest. He has a degree in Classical Guitar from UNM, and a degree in English. He teaches in Monterey, California. He is working on opening a conservatory of music in Monterey. He has three children.

Louis Martin lived only three days but is never forgotten.

ORDINATION

Chapter 58

I waited for many days hoping for the mailman to bring me news to know if I had been chosen for the Deacon Program. At last, the letter of Acceptance arrived and, I thanked God for choosing me to serve him. However: later about three weeks before ordination I injured myself moving a washing machine and, I thought that there was no way that I could be ordained, but in a dream, I saw myself wearing an Alb which is the garment worn by a Deacon when he serves at Mass and, again God showed me that he is in charge.

A deacon usually has several ministries he must assist in, even before being ordained. I had been with the Society of St. Vincent de Paul for many years, at one time President of the Holy Name Society, later as well as RCIA Co-Ordinator. But the main source of nourishment for all deacons is God's Word and administering the Holy Eucharist to the sick and infirmed. For many years I took Holy Communion to patients at a Nursing Home It is Christ whom we serve. Like the seven deacons the Apostles first selected, we too have been chosen by God to serve His people.

Saint Paul tells us "There many ministries but the same Lord" (1 Corinthians 12:5). In this vein we work in various assignments as directed by the bishop and working under the Pastor or Vicar of the Parish.

I was Ordained by Archbishop Michael Sheehan on June 26, 1993, as a Permanent Deacon at Queen of Heaven Parish where

I was assigned to serve. I was in a class with forty-seven Candidates. From an educational evaluation I was number 11 in the group as decided by the Deacon Training Staff. It was Archbishop Sheehan who presided at my anniversary Mass for my fifty years as a member of the Secular Order of Mount Carmel Order in 2005. Present for this celebration were other priests, Deacons and wives of the Archdiocese of Santa Fe, Liturgy Team of Queen of Heaven Parish, Combined Choirs, The Carmelites Nuns of Santa Fe and Queen of Heaven Parishioners. My family and friends were present. It was a joyous time for me and all who attended.

Since then, I have been active in my parish as Spiritual Advisor to the Conference of Saint Vincent De Paul with which I had been working for many years. The Saint Vincent De Paul Society is a world-wide Organization serving the poor. In 1953 I started the Conference at Holy Rosary Parish where I belonged at the time. We started with four members and served the people of that parish for many years. My wife and I fed people at my home. We were allowed by the Pastor Father Hammer to serve donuts on Sunday after mass to raise funds for our work. Today during this Epidemic of Covid -19 we cannot visit persons in their own home, but we provide them with gift cards to purchase groceries and other needs.

I was asked by one of the Catholic Daughters when I was first ordained to be their Chaplain. I have been their Chaplain for 28 years. The Chaplain presides at the installation of officers and conducts a spiritual presentation on a monthly date. The Catholic Daughters are a vital presence in the parish providing funds for the Seminary for the training of priests, contributing to the Saint Vincent de Paul Conference, Catholic Charities, and other services. It is a joy to be associated with such a wonderful group of women. They wear special garments on occasion which make them stand out.

I began the RCIA which is an acronym for Rite of Christian Initiation of Adults in my parish at the request of our

Pastor at the time. I started with one non-baptized person for instructions and the following week she brought her non-baptized friend and by the time of Easter we had 6 persons to join the Church, and later we had as many as 22 persons joining the Church.

I was appointed Spiritual Assistant to the Secular Carmelites in Albuquerque by the Provincial in California Father Donald Kinney. The Rule says that a Carmelite priest must be the Assistant, but if one is not available then another priest may be selected. The community could not find a priest to replace the one that retired, so I was appointed.

My work involves presiding at the reception of Promises of the candidates and, interviewing them before being admitted to the order. I do a presentation monthly on a subject of a Carmelite Saint or relating to prayer and contemplation. We have a community that is dedicated to the Order and, we are growing as many people are searching for greater meaning in their lives. The Carmelite Order offers a Rule that dates back centuries and leads people to a relationship with Christ.

Anniversary Mass For Deacon Ruben Barela

Fifty Years as a Secular Carmelite Order of Discalced Carmelites

Spiritual Assistant to Carmel

Twice I was appointed as Spiritual Assistant for the Holy Cross Community in Albuquerque. The Rule states that a priest of the Order must be the Spiritual Assistant or if not available a Secular priest may be named, but after making many calls we could not find a priest, consequently the community got permission from the Provincial to allow me to carry on the duty.

It is the duty of the Assistant to interview the candidates for their First Promise and to prepare a talk on Carmelite topics for the benefit of the community. I love the Carmelite Order and its history, its charism, its Saints, the Priests that serve us, the Nuns, Brothers, Deacons, and others who contribute to this great community of contemplatives who do all for the good of, the Church. We trace our Order to Saint Elijah not historically but spiritually. I wish that more men would answer the call to be contemplatives, because in our community the women make up eighty percent of the community. By being a contemplative, a person becomes more aware of the supernatural life, more aware of the importance of silent prayer, of fraternal virtue, of the thirst for a relationship with God and our Blessed Mother of Mount Carmel.

Secular Order Discalced Carmelites
Office of Provincial Delegate Western Region
P.O. Box 3079   San Jose CA 95156-3079 (408) 251-1361

APPOINTMENT OF SPIRITUAL ASSISTANT

Name: Deacon Ruben Barela, ocds Address: 3131 Truman NE
City: Albuquerque State: NM Zip: 87110
Telephone: (505) 872-2617
Appointed to OCDS: Albuquerque, New Mexico Community/~~Group~~

"The Spiritual Assistant to each community is usually a friar of the Order. His duty is to give spiritual aid to the community so that its members may be guided in their vocation and may correspond with it as perfectly as possible. He will also endeavor to promote solidarity between the secular community and the friars and the nuns of the Order. At the invitation of the Council he may attend meetings of the Council, without having a right to vote. At the different stages of formation of the candidates, he will be available to interview them. The Council may consult him about the suitability of the candidate to assume the responsibility of the vocation to the Secular Order. He will support the formation of the community by his availability to the Director of Formation. ...The Spiritual Assistant must be well versed in Carmelite spirituality and well-informed in the Church's teaching concerning the role of lay people in the Church." (O.C.D.S. Constitutions #44)

In addition to the duties outlined above in #44 the spiritual assistant:

1. Attends the monthly meeting.
2. Prepares and delivers a spiritual conference to the Community / Group each month according to the outline of topics mutually agreed upon with the Council.
3. Celebrates the Eucharist if it is possible and opportune.
4. Accepts candidates into Formation, and receives the Promises and Vows of the members in the name of the Order and signs the appropriate forms. (When necessary he may delegate this duty)

This appointment is being made of the above stated person with the understanding that the person accepts the duties and obligations of being a spiritual assistant in the Secular Order of Discalced Carmelites, and has the permission of his/her superior. This person is hereby appointed to that same office as of: May 24, 2017. This office expires upon the appointment of a successor.

Name: Fr. Donald Kinney, OCD Date: May 24, 2017
Provincial Delegate for OCDS

cc: Council and Spiritual Assistant   Rev. 1/12

Man of God

In my work with Saint Vincent De Paul there some needy people who found out where I lived and when others refused to help them, they would come to me. There was a neighbor who lived not far from me who would bring homeless people to me so that I could help them. One of the ladies who had several children would come even at night asking for money to buy milk and other food. One day I asked her why are you coming to me? She said, "because you are a man of God." I believe that those who help the needy are men and women of God. "Amen, I say to you, whatever you did for one of these least brothers of mine you did for me"[32]

Keeping the Faith

Continuing education is paramount in our spiritual growth. The reading of Scripture, attending workshops, retreats, meditation, and contemplative prayer are a must. Serving at liturgy is another highlight of a deacon's life. Proclaiming the Gospel and preaching is an important element in the Holy Mass. It takes much prayer and silence to prepare for these duties. Earnest and humble supplication to the Holy Spirit provides the inspiration before delivering a homily to a congregation. It takes a good deal of time and lonely effort to put it all together. But the results pay off. We are all grateful to those who worked so hard in Vatican II deliberations to restore the Catholic diaconate.

The Carmelite Priests

The Carmelites Priests were also active in our spiritual journey conducting retreats, workshops and providing spiritual direction, among them were Father John Michael Payne, Father Anthony Morello, Father Bonaventure, and many others. They practice and teach Carmelites contemplative prayer. They work in some of the oldest Churches in California some founded be Early Irish Priests and Saint Junipero Serra. They follow the teachings of our Carmelite Saints and the teachings of Our Catholic Church.

THE GREAT PARISH ROBBERY

Chapter 59

How could this happen? On Monday after Christmas, 2014, I assisted at Mass, as is normal in my role as deacon. After Mass it was my duty that day to open the safe and take the money bags to the counters at the parish office about two blocks away, near Queen of Heaven School. It was Monday after Christmas the school was closed. Everyone had left after Mass except for a man and his wife, a couple of faithful parishioners. The man's name is Dick. He was a Mayordomo one that prepares the Altar and lights the candles before Mass.

As I exited the back door of the church with money bags in hand, a car drove up and blocked my car from backing out. Dick's wife was already in their pick-up which was parked next to me. The men that were blocking my car got out of their car and began talking to Dick. I suspected something bad, because they had blocked my car from backing out of my parking space. Dick was talking to the men, and I asked him "What do they want?" He answered that they were looking for the Veteran's Hospital. The other fellow kept staring at me and appeared to have something in his coat pocket. I thought it might be a knife.

Dick suffered a form of dementia and could not remember the name of the street adjacent to the Church. I broke in on the conversation and gave them directions to the Hospital. They then returned to their car and left. Dick and his wife drove off and I thought to myself, "Well, we took care of that," but I was totally unprepared for what happened next.

I drove my car over to the Church office and parked in one of the regular parking spaces. Suddenly, and before I could exit, the same two men in the car drove up and again blocked my car from any movement as I had parked next to the school building.

One of them got out, came over to my car and tapped on the window. I pushed the button to lower it, but only slightly. I guess I held the button down too long so that it went down all the way. Then the fellow lunged at me, full-force, and tried to grab my keys. I struggled with him, but at a definite disadvantage since he was standing while I still sat in my car; he was a very strong young man.

Now of the attack, he was able to wrest the keys away from me, quickly open the trunk of the car and snatch the money bags. I struggled to exit feeling pain in my right hand. Finally managing to get out of my car, I attempted to grab the perpetrators' car door which was still open, but he was able to get in and they sped away.

I went into the office and told the receptionist that I had been robbed. She called police and reported what had happened. They responded quickly and arrived at our office almost immediately. When one officer saw my swollen right hand, he told me to get to a hospital right away. One of our receptionists drove me to Urgent Care. It took several doctor visits before my hand would properly heal.

We lost all the cash from the Christmas collection and the weekend money also. Later it was learned that the thieves had abandoned the car they were driving and stole another to make yet another getaway. The robbery was reported on TV, radio, and newspaper, but we never heard if the criminals had been apprehended.

As ministers and servants of our Church, we are always in

need of God's protection. I believe that Our Blessed Mother was watching over me that day.

A few weeks later another Deacon was killed by robbers who robbed him and dragged him with their car as he tried to prevent them from getting away. The men who robbed me were not from our country. I believe they were from Mexico and so were those who robbed the other deacon.

<u>Thou Shalt not Kill.</u>

Many years after the war a priest said to me after Mass, "since you were in the war tell me, you do not have to answer the question if you do not want, but what do you think…should the person go to confession if having killed an enemy combatant in war? I answered: "usually, the Chaplain with the permission of the bishop can give "Absolution" to a group of men going into battle with the idea of confessing any serious sin at the first opportunity." "Absolution" is a power given to the priest in the Catholic Church to forgive sin.

That is all I said, but I kept wondering, how did this priest whom I barely knew, know to ask me such a question? I had never told him that I was in the war. Perhaps my age gave him a clue that I was in World War II. I thought that killing someone in battle was not a sin, so I did not confess it, that is until this priest asked me the question. I kept pondering did I confess it before. I could not remember ever confessing it. About three weeks later I did confess that as a first scout I had to kill to defend myself and the two-hundred soldiers fifty yards behind me in the jungle.

It was my duty as a first scout to check the huts on the side of the road as recorded in my story "The Lonely Road." The Catechism of the Catholic Church states: "Legitimate defense is a grave duty for whoever is responsible for the lives of others or the common good" (CCC # 2321)[33]. I could have skipped some of these stories to make me look good, but I must stand before God at my death and the truth is the truth. He calls us not because we are perfect but because he loves us beyond anything of this earth. I hope that my brother Deacons and other faithful will not think of me as cruel, but God knows I did my best to serve others. I have tried to preach the Gospel with clarity and truth. The Prophet Isaiah says: "How beautiful on the mountain are the feet of those who preach the Good News to the poor" (Isaiah 52:7).

EPILOGUE

As I underwent pilot training my instructor often commented upon the need to trust the instruments. He explained that man is not in his natural environment when in the air. Your body will lie to you. Your aircraft may be flying straight and level, while your body keeps making you feel you are in a turn. Such information is easy to ignore when you see the horizon and the terrain. It is when you can't see; that the instruments are critical for survival.

In life, we often ignore that which makes us uncomfortable. We make choices based upon how we believe things will play out. We lack the instrumentation to help us navigate. Instead, we stumble our way through life. In this book the instrumentation for life is revealed. Faith in God, faith in the Church, and faith in a community.

Throughout his life, the right course was often obscured by hardship, war, business stress, and family conflict. By holding fast to the fundamentals learned as a Catholic child while under the care of the Sisters of St Francis, a fruitful and meaningful life was achieved. Now, at the age of 99, the author is still ministering to the Secular Carmelites as their Spiritual Assistant, and, as Chaplain to the Catholic Daughters Court 2310 at Queen of Heaven Parish. He assists at Mass on Sundays and preaches once a month, the reader is encouraged to explore the Catholic Church. It offers a doctrine, it offers sacraments, it offers itself as map to navigate a course to God.

By Paul Barela

BACK COVER COMMENTARY

graphics by Kelli MacPhail Gómez, Minnie P. Dávila, Brookelyn Resecker

The scene for my book is life itself. I am writing for all people, although deacons, priests, religious, may find value in it, others in the military, and ordinary people will perhaps feel a common thread that touches their existence because I write not only about my war experience, but my trials in marriage my wife's mental illness, and prayer life. The first part of the book lays a foundation for the latter part where the nugget can be found. It has taken me almost four years to write this book. It centers on my faith in God beginning at Saint Anthony's Orphanage where I spent nine years of my young age. I continued to practice my faith by going to Mass, and a simple prayer life when I left the orphanage. Somehow the family was able to survive the turbulent years of the Crash of 29. My school years were much the same as other boys of that age and time. In 1943 I volunteered for the Army when World War II was raging. I was trained for warfare in the South Pacific where I had some unusual experiences as a first scout in the jungles of Bougainville and other islands. I survived due to my faith in God. When the war was over, I got a job, married, had seven children joined the Carmelite Order and was ordained a Deacon in 1993.

Deacon Ruben J. Barela

AFTERWARD

<u>Pope Saint John Paul and Carmel</u>

Pope Saint John Paul wrote a small booklet called "Prayer and Carmel," " When prayer resulting from the stronger action of the love of God shows signs of a close friendship with God and reaches the point that it is a relationship or union of love- the friendship then becomes an apostolic leaven, a cause of joy to the Church and to men, as if it was a powerful voice reaching to the heart of God for the good of all people."

Pope Francis' on the Deacons – May 2020

The deacon is not a second hand - priest. He is part of the clergy.

He is a servant of the Word and the poor. He proclaims the Word of God at Mass.

In serving the poor he sees the face of Christ.

May deacons be an invigorating symbol to the entire Church.

(You – Tube – Vatican-News – May 2020)

BIBLIOGRAPHY

[1] *Catechism of the Catholic Church.* (n.d.). New York: Doubleday Publishing; pg26

[2] (Romans10: v 17, New American Bible – A Saint Joseph Edition, Catholic Book Publishing Corp. New Jersey).

[3] (Isaiah 7: v. 14, The New American Bible-Catholic Biblical Association 1969).

[4] (Genesis 8, v. 1, New American Bible, A Saint Joseph Edition, Catholic Book Publishing Corp. New Jersey)

[5] ("Four Hundred Years of Faith," Archbishop of Santa Fe Michael J. Sheehan)

[6] (Catechism of the Catholic Church, p.174-part one, LK22, - 19)

[7] (Mathew: 14, v. 25-31, New American Bible, A Saint Joseph Edition, Catholic Book Publishing Corp. New Jersey).

[8] (JN: 15: v. 14-15, New Testament of New American Bible, Saint Joseph Edition, Catholic Book Publishing Co. New York}.

[9] (Catechism of the Catholic Church, # 525)

[10] (LK: v. 27-29, 31-32-New Testament of the New American Bible, Saint Joseph Edition, Catholic Book Publishing Co., New York)

[11] (James 4: v 12, NAB, Saint Joseph Edition, Catholic Book Publishing Co. New York)

[12] (Baltimore Catechism)

[13] (1. Book of Kings, v. 10-14, v. 20-23, New American Bible, St. Joseph Edition, Catholic Book Publishing Corp> New Jersey}

[14] (Discalced Carmelite website:. Discalced Carmelites) or https://www.discalcedcarmelites.org

[15] (Collected Works of Saint John of the Cross. Kieran Kavanaugh, OCD and Otilio Rodrigues, OCD)

[16] ("My Sister Saint Therese" Tan Books and Publishing, Inc. 1997)

[17] (LK: 22: 31-32) New American Bible, A Saint Joseph Edition, Catholic Book Publishing Corp. New Jersey

[18] (NAB9-St. Joseph Edition)

[19] (Lectio Divina and the Practice of Teresian Prayer, Sam Anthony Morello, OCD, ICS Publications, Washington, DC)

[20] "(Spiritual Canticle" -16: v Collected Works of Saint John of the Cross) (Kieran Kavanaugh and Otilio Rodriguez)

[21] (Our Sunday Visitor, Inc, Oct. 1978)

[22] (St. Therese of Lisieux by those who knew her – Our Sunday Visitor. Oct. 1978)

[23] (St. Therese of Lisieux by those who Knew her – Our Sunday Visitor, Inc.-1978)

[24] (My Sister St. Therese-Tan Books and Publishers, Inc. 1997).

[25] (Our Sunday Visitor Inc.-1978).

[26] (Infant Jesus of Prague – Wikipedia, the free encyclopedia).

[27] (The Way of Vincent De Paul, Robert P. Maloney, C.M., New City Press)

[28] New American Bible, St Joseph Edition, Catholic Book Publishing Corp, New Jersey

[29] (Chapter 16 – The Collected Works of Saint John of the Cross, Kieran Kavanauh and Otilio Rodriguez)

[30] ("The Collected Works of St. John of the Cross" Kieran Kavanaugh, OCD, Otilio Rodriguez, OCD. The Spiritual Canticle, chapter 16, Paragraph 6)

[31] (The Life of Saint Teresa of Jesus, XXXII P. 300-332 -The Autobiography -translated and edited by E. Allison Peers -Image Books-A Division of Doubleday & Company, Garden City, New York).

[32] (Mathew: 25, v 40, New American Bible, St. Joseph Edition, Catholic Book Publishing Corp., New Jersey)

[33] www.scborromeo.org/ccc/para/2321.htm

ABBREVIATIONS

aka	Also Known As
BAR	Browning Automatic Rifle.
CCC	Catholic Catechism of the Church www.scborromeo.org/ccc/para/2321.htm
CM	Congregation of the Mission
OCD	Order of Carmelites Discalced
OCDS	Secular Order of Discalced Carmelites
PNM	Public Service Company of New Mexico
RCIA	Right of Christian Initiation for Adults

UNM   University of New Mexico
WPA   Works Progress Administration

ABOUT THE AUTHOR

Deacon Ruben Barela lives in Albuquerque, New Mexico and was Ordained in 1993 by Archbishop Michael J. Sheehan. He was married for thirty- nine- years to Consuelo Parra and had seven children. Although not receiving a college degree he took classes at the College of Santa Fe and UNM in Albuquerque on philosophy, Counseling, Foundations of Education, English, Spanish in addition to theology and religious studies from the faculty of the Diaconate Program from The Archdiocese of Santa Fe. He has continued his education in homiletics and teaching for many years.

Deacon Barela strongly believes in financially supporting our Seminaries. He urges his readers to do likewise. It is essential to keep reinforcing those on the front lines.

Made in the USA
Columbia, SC
14 October 2024

43548436R00104